OUTWIT
THE WORKPLACE
BULLY

8 STEPS YOU NEED TO KNOW TO RECLAIM
YOUR CAREER, CONFIDENCE, AND SANITY

DAWN M. JOHNSON

Outwit the Workplace Bully: 8 Steps You Need to Know to Reclaim Your Career, Confidence, and Sanity
© Copyright 2021 by Dawn M. Johnson, MAM, MBA

ISBN: 979-8-9852132-0-1 (paperback)
ISBN: 979-8-9852132-1-8 (ebook)

Editors: Val Cervarich and Carly Catt
Cover Design: Natasja Storm,. Cutting Edge Studio
Formatting: Arjen Broeze, Kingfisher Design
Writing Coach: Kerk Murray
Author Photograph: Three Irish Girls Photography

For speaking engagements or consulting services, contact the author at info@ontherisedevelopment.com

www.ontherisedevelopment.com

Before you begin...

Your FREE companion workbook is one click away!

To get the most out of this book, I've created a companion workbook that you can download now! I've found readers who utilize the workbook can implement next steps and experience freedom from bullying much more quickly than those who don't.

The workbook is packed with reflection aids, templates, and bonus content to enhance your reading and learning experience.

Claim your copy by scanning the QR-code below:

Dedication

To my parents, Norman Johnson, and the late Karen Johnson, who supported me through the toughest situations, gave me strength to stand strong in the face of injustice, and most importantly, taught me to always be kind.

A Note
from the Author

As I was selecting a title for this book, some believed I shouldn't use the word bully. Their reasoning ranged from "it sounds childish" to "no one will pick it up because it means admitting they're weak."

I agree. The word *bully* feels childish. I also agree that in the past, admitting that you had been bullied as an adult typically left an impression of weakness. For both reasons, I dislike the word bully. A lot. Some advocates have suggested better terms might be *psychological violence,* or *nonstatus harassment.* The term bully doesn't convey the seriousness of the offense. Perhaps its very name prevents it from being recognized as a harmful act.

All that said, *workplace bullying* is the most common term used by academic researchers and human resource officials to describe the behavior I am referencing, which is why I use that term throughout the book.

Every effort has been made to hide the identity of the bullies in my stories. Gender neutral pronouns (i.e., they and them) are used to further mask the aggressors' genders. I chose to intentionally conceal identities not because extreme misbehavior shouldn't be admonished but because disgracing the offenders isn't my goal. Targeting the bullies sends me down to their level, making me no better than them. Sharing what I have learned and helping others is more important than embarrassing the bullies.

The locations where my experiences occurred are anonymized as well. One experience occurred in a large university outside of my home state. For clarification, this incident *did not* occur at my beloved alma mater, The College of St. Scholastica. I mention this to ensure that no harm comes to the college's reputation. My second experience took place in a professional workplace.

I use the word *professional* throughout my book to refer to the targets of bullying incidents. Many of my examples are set in an office given my personal experiences. I don't intend to leave people with the impression that workplace bullying only occurs in an office setting or within certain professions. Workplace bullying can (and does) occur in college classrooms, corporate board rooms, restaurant kitchens, manufacturing floors, construction sites, hospital wards, retail stores, and anywhere else a bully finds employment. No industry or profession is immune to the perils of the workplace bully. Bullying even occurs in remote work environments. My use of the term *professional* refers to anyone who is employed, regardless of their role or industry.

By sharing my stories and knowledge, my intention is to empower readers like you to take next steps toward a safer, more fulfilling workplace experience. The psychological trauma of workplace bullying is real. I'm not a psychologist or mental health professional. The advice provided in this book is based on my experience and should not be used as a replacement for professional mental health support. The story details may be anonymized, but I'm certain you'll see yourself and others in my descriptions. Know that you're not alone, and a bully-free life is within reach.

Table of Contents

Introduction

I'm happy you're here. But I'm sorry we had to meet this way.

If you're reading this book, it means that you and I share a common experience—one that we don't often talk about. It's an experience that changed the trajectory of our careers and maybe even our lives. You and I belong to the group of millions of people who experience the nightmare of workplace bullying each year. We thought we left the bullies behind in grade school. Yet we've encountered a more sophisticated and diabolical form of bullying at work. This book was written by me, for you, from one target to another.

Workplace bullies are not just teasing you. They are not just trying to hurt your feelings. They are going after the very things that you value most in your professional life. They are out to tarnish your reputation and derail your career. They attack your ability to make a living and endanger your financial security.

In the process of trying to protect your livelihood, you experience emotional, mental, and physical exhaustion. Your performance suffers. Your health suffers. Your relationships suffer. The result is the complete disruption of your life. You may continue to suffer the impacts of your encounter long after you leave the bully behind.

My incidents with workplace bullying led me to a career in leadership development. I believed that if I could work to create strong leaders, less bullying would occur. After ten years in the field, I still felt like I was hardly making a dent. Every week, I heard another story from a friend, family member, or colleague about a leader who was abusive or who had allowed abusive behavior to continue under their watch.

In the months before deciding to write this book, several friends pointed out that the leaders who really needed my guidance would never seek it (at least not willingly). While I was helping good leaders to become better leaders, I was never going to motivate the abusive to be less abusive.

A moment of clarity occurred when I was featured on the

Wellness Renaissance Podcast. As the host and I talked, she shared a negative experience she'd had in the workplace. After I gave her some advice, she laughed and said, "Where were you back then? I needed you back then!"

Eureka! This conversation with a woman I had just met gave me the clarity I needed. While I had been investing time to support leaders for the last ten years, who was supporting all the employees who struggled to deal with bullying leaders and colleagues? I realized that I was in a unique position to help those who had encountered bullying and other abuses in the workplace. I am not uniquely qualified to help other targets because of my degree in psychology or because I work in human resources or because I've developed leaders for more than a decade. I'm uniquely qualified because I've been targeted not once but twice by workplace bullies.

My two experiences exposed me to different types of bullying tactics, and I learned how bullies leverage their network of helpers to further their agenda. I had to fight to maintain my professional reputation and to secure a new position with my career and finances intact. During both of my experiences, my confidence was crushed, and I was mentally and emotionally drained. I had to claw my way back to a healthy and confident place. I've lived with self-blame and shame. I navigated strong feelings like anger, vengeance, and grief, and I had to work through the emotions to move forward in my life. I endured the feeling of isolation you might be facing. I comprehend the fear that people won't believe your story, or they'll believe that you did something to bring the abuse on yourself. This book helps you realize what you are experiencing is real and that it isn't your fault.

My guidance will apply to both those who are currently in a bullying situation and those who have navigated out of a past situation. If you are currently being targeted by a bully in your workplace, I encourage you to leave. I provide recommendations about the things you should consider and prepare before you exit. If you were bullied in a previous position, I'll help you build your Bully Intelligence and move into your future with confidence.

This book is for people who want to move away from the abuse. If you are looking for a book on how to "get along" with the bully at work, you'll be disappointed. Likewise, I won't give a ton of advice about working through your organizational channels. Why? From my personal experiences, my research, and what I have learned from talking with other targets, the bully rarely changes, the bully is rarely punished, and human resources is often unprepared (or untrained) to deal with these situations. The result is rarely favorable for the target.

The bully has stolen enough of your time, energy, and life. It's time to stop thinking about what's going on, worrying about your future, and fearing every day at work. Are you ready to physically move out of the bully's reach? Or are you ready to loosen the emotional hold your encounter still has on your life? Don't let one more day go by without learning how to leave the bully behind.

The eight-step process I've created will help you break free both mentally and physically from the bully. Each chapter dives into a step, supporting you to build and master the knowledge and skills needed to defend yourself and your career. As you move through the eight steps, I have three goals for you. One, I want to help you build what I call your *Bully Intelligence,* or your ability to quickly recognize behaviors synonymous with workplace bullies. Developing your Bully Intelligence will help you (and you will be able to help others) in future workplaces should you encounter another aggressor. Two, I want you to put the practical tips into action immediately. At the end of each chapter, I've included reflection questions and exercises. I encourage you to take a few minutes after each chapter and examine your experience in relation to the concepts covered. Finally, I want you to feel hopeful, encouraged, and strong again. By the time you reach the end of the book, I want you to feel inspired to move forward on your journey and leave the bully behind.

Outlined below are the eight steps we'll explore together.

Step One – Recognizing the Signs.
Are you being targeted by a bully? When you can recognize the signs and behaviors of a bully early, you can better protect your career and reputation from damage. During this step, you will learn about types of workplace bullies, the behaviors to look for, and the characteristics of the typical target.

Step Two – Navigating the Chaos.

This step offers a deep dive into the bullying process. Fully develop your Bully Intelligence by learning about the targeting stages and about the bully's network of helpers and bystanders.

Step Three – Containing Emotions.

The bully counts on your emotional reaction to their abusive treatment. Your reaction can (and often does) impact your ability to be successful in the job. This step covers the ways bullies use your own emotions against you and ways to keep yourself emotionally grounded.

Step Four – Maintaining Mental Health.

The range of emotions that targets experience is vast—fear, anxiety, anger, shame, and grief are all common reactions. Through this step, you'll discover techniques you can put into practice immediately to reduce the impact on your mental health. Learn the importance of having both an informal support system along with professional mental health support.

Step Five – Protecting Your Career.

When you make the decision to leave the bully behind, there are steps you need to take both before you leave your position and as you prepare to enter a new workplace. In this step, learn how to document your experience and achievements, what information you need to gather before you leave, how to prepare for an exit interview, and things to consider as you prepare for your new workplace and coworkers.

Step Six – Believing in Yourself.

Rebuilding your confidence and restoring your resilience are important steps in the healing process. This step discusses how to purge the words the bully put in your head, utilize self-care as a part of the restoration process, and recognize the strength your experience has provided.

Step Seven – Letting Go.
Being able to forgive is a significant step in letting go of the mental anguish the bully inflicts. This step covers the importance of forgiveness in moving forward, how to identify and assimilate the lessons from your encounter, and even how to generate gratitude for your experience.

Step Eight – Telling Your Story.
Targets have spent too much time under a cloud of shame and self-blame. Telling your story can be empowering to you and inspiring to others. In this final step, you'll learn the power of your story.

Before we can get into the steps, you need to understand my story. In the chapter called "Setting the Stage," you'll learn about my two bullying experiences. The encounters exhibit very different bullies, and they occurred years apart in two separate workplaces. It's important to start with these stories because I reference both throughout the book to illustrate key points.

My path to this moment of sharing my experience started in 1995. At that time, I never set out to become an experiential expert on workplace bullying. No one does. But I'm grateful that I can now share what I have learned with you. Thank you for allowing me to lead you through this process and into a hope-filled and bully-free future.

Setting the Stage

My Experience with Workplace Bullying

Nothing has impacted my career trajectory more than my encounters with workplace bullies. But the impact has not been all negative. Truthfully, I would say that almost all of the twists and turns I took have been positive. Thanks to my experiences, I have a satisfying career, a thriving consulting practice, and a strong professional reputation. Heck, I even wrote a book!

Yet when I was in those moments with the bullies, all I could see was the negative. All I was focused on was the pain, the fear, and the struggle. It took years of reflection, healing, learning, and trial and error to unearth the nuggets of value.

One of the nuggets I dug up was the importance of telling my story. As I conceptualized this book, I knew immediately that I would include a chapter on telling your own story. The final chapter, Step Eight, focuses on that concept exclusively.

For many years, though, I didn't tell my story. In fact, many friends and colleagues are hearing my story for the first time through this book. Until recent years, I shared my story somewhat selectively. I might have shared parts to sympathize with a colleague who was going through a similar experience. Or I shared my stories with close friends to illustrate why I might react to or feel a certain way about something. It wasn't until I started to share my story more fully that I unlocked its true power. Friends who hid their own experiences opened up to me and finally realized they were not alone. Then I started to get requests for advice about dealing with bullying and other toxic behavior in the workplace.

Please note that as I tell my stories, I'm doing my part

to maintain anonymity for the involved parties. You'll see me referencing to the bullies as *they, the supervisor,* or *the boss.* This has been part of my processing of the events and can boost your confidence about what's possible as you might choose to share your story in the future.

Sharing a story about a vulnerable time in your life can be scary, but I have found it amazingly liberating. These workplace bullying stories have shaped me and have become a part of who I am. I share these experiences from a place of hope and empowerment to prepare you for your journey ahead.

The Graduate School Bully

My first year after college, I worked as a research assistant in a graduate program at a large midwestern university. The signs that my supervisor was an aggressor showed up in the first weeks in the program. Although, being a bit naive and new to the "real world of work" at the time, I misunderstood many of the indicators.

I would describe my supervisor's personality as generally negative and unhappy. That fact in and of itself doesn't necessarily make them a bully or a bad supervisor. What categorizes their behavior as abuse is the broader pattern of their words and behaviors. As I relay the story, see if you can spot the behaviors and patterns that may categorize them as a bully.

When things didn't go as planned, my supervisor would make comments to the group of research assistants like this: "I thought you could handle this without my supervision, but I guess not" or "I guess this is what happens when I delegate." The supervisor continually reminded us that the good work that had been done on the project was not from our efforts but from the hard work of the previous group of research assistants.

It was a common occurrence for our supervisor to work from home. They would assure us they'd be available for questions, but when we reached out, they rarely answered the call or returned the message. When the inability to get questions answered caused a work delay (or an error), it was the research assistant's fault, not the supervisor's.

They'd often tell us we needed to be in the office by 8 a.m.

ready to work, but once there, we'd wait (often for hours) for the supervisor to get their portion of the work done so we could start on ours. Our work still needed to be completed that day regardless of what we had going on or how late we needed to stay. The supervisor would frequently declare, "You owe me [number] hours."

Little problems or issues would be blown out of proportion and often result in long meetings where the research assistants were berated for their mistakes. After the meetings, we'd often learn that the mistake wasn't a big deal and only took a matter of minutes to fix.

Shortly after starting in this role, my supervisor's attention landed squarely on me. They would frequently embarrass me in meetings by saying things like, "Thanks to Dawn, you'll have to repeat the test. She screwed up." On one occasion, they blamed me for the entire team not hitting a statistical milestone. I found out later that it wasn't my fault. The problem was the way the supervisor had conducted the test.

In another incident, I became ill with strep throat and missed a training session. My supervisor wouldn't allow me to take my earned sick day. Instead, I had to make up the day. The make-up day happened to fall on the Friday before a holiday weekend. A day I had planned to travel home. Because I missed the training, I also had to complete the training exercise three times, while those who were at the training only had to complete it once.

Is this what the real world is like? Is this adult behavior? I wasn't sure what was going on, but I knew that I didn't like working for this supervisor. What *was* occurring soon became clear after another research assistant came into my office one day. I will never forget that conversation. My fellow research assistant said, "I'm sorry, Dawn. Every year [the supervisor] chooses someone to single out and pick on. It looks like this year that person is you."

I was stunned. They went on to tell me that during the previous year, the supervisor drove the only male student out of the program.

Another research assistant approached me a couple of weeks later and apologized for not being able to help or defend me. They explained that they were in the final stages of their dissertation and the data from the project we were working on was critical for their research. They feared that if they stood up for me, they would lose access to the information needed to complete their PhD program. They couldn't risk restarting years of research.

My grad school colleagues were not calling the supervisor's behavior bullying. It would be years before I even learned that term. They did, however, recognize a pattern of behavior from what they'd witnessed before.

As you read how examples and tips relate to this story, I use the terms "grad school bully" or "grad school experience."

Perhaps when you think about a bully, you think of someone like my grad school supervisor—angry, critical, and threatening. However, workplace bullies come in many forms. In my next story, you'll see that some bullies are much more devious and deceptive.

The Workplace Bully

My second encounter with workplace bullying occurred more than a decade after my first experience. Unlike in grad school where I knew there was an angry and negative personality in my midst, the behavior from this second incident appeared out of nowhere. Eventually, I came to realize that the bully had been targeting me for months. Despite learning some lessons from my previous bullying experience, I had not yet fully developed my Bully Intelligence. I was unable to detect that someone was working behind the scenes to destroy my career and reputation until it was too late.

Years into my career, I found myself in a leadership role. My position was sometimes exhausting, but I loved my job. The variety challenged me, and days flew by. On paydays, I often forgot that I actually got paid to do my work. I was confident that I was good at my job and well-respected by my colleagues.

On the day of my annual performance evaluation, I had no fears. I had a good relationship with my boss, and despite a challenging year, I'd hit my overall milestones, secured additional funding for my program, and improved client outcomes.

My boss asked me what I thought had gone well during the year, and I relayed a few of my bigger accomplishments. Then they said, "Well, here is what didn't go well. You have no leadership ability, no vision for your area, no management skills…"

After these first few statements, I laughed because I thought they were kidding. But I could tell from the seriousness on their face that they were not: "You throw your title around, you can't get along with your coworkers, and you struggle, in general, to represent the organization well." By the time they got to the end of the list, tears were streaming down my face.

I had no idea where all this criticism had come from. They had given me no negative feedback throughout the year. They went on to say, "I'm hiring a new director to replace you. You can stay on and do administrative work." I was devastated. I stated that I was very sorry and that the last thing I wanted to do was disappoint anyone. I told them that I wanted to work harder and show them that I was deserving of my position. They didn't seem to care.

They asked if I agreed with my review and put the back page down in front of me and told me to sign it. I didn't agree with them, but at the time I didn't think I had a choice. Through bleary eyes, I reluctantly signed my name. I asked if I could keep a copy, so I could review the items they wanted me to work on. They said they would give me a copy within a couple of days.

I went back to my office, straightened myself out, touched up my makeup, and worked the rest of the day. I said nothing to my coworkers. I never let anyone know there was anything wrong.

Despite threatening to demote me, weeks went by and nothing happened. My boss rarely spoke to me or even looked at me as we passed in the hallway. But I started to notice a pattern. Every couple of weeks, they would come into my office and be angry. They would say something like "I guess I can't let you do [task]." Perplexed, I would ask why. Their response was almost always, "I just can't." They never told me why they were angry or the details around their decision to remove work from my purview.

This happened multiple times over several months. I began

to suspect that someone must be telling my boss things about me that weren't true. I couldn't believe that any of my coworkers would tell lies about me. I also couldn't imagine that my boss would act on those statements without checking with me first.

Months into this pattern, my boss came in once again, upset and ready to remove me from another initiative. At this point I had had it. I was tired of being accused, I was tired of not being able to defend myself, and I was tired of the conflict. I decided I would take a risk. Very calmly, I said, "I am not sure why you are upset. I'm not doing or saying anything that should make you this angry." Then I started to say, "It feels like someone is telling you things that are not true—"

They cut me off, leaned over my desk, and yelled, "People tell me what you say, Dawn!"

I'm not sure what my boss said after that except that at one point they stopped ranting and asked, "Are you okay?" I weakly responded yes. I am sure that all the blood had drained from my face as I sat in disbelief. *Someone had been telling my boss things that were not true ... but who?*

At that point, I had no idea who was working to sabotage me, but I knew that they had somehow convinced my boss to threaten to demote me. It would be months before I would get closer to the truth. It would be years before I understood how little my performance review had to do with my actual performance and my boss's threats. What I did know was that this was probably not going to get better and that I needed to find a new job as soon as possible. I mobilized myself and all my resources to make that transition.

I'm fully aware that unless you have experienced this type of manipulative bully, you may think my story is pure fiction. Let me affirm that this type of bullying encounter is more common than you would believe.

This story involves more than one bully. Maybe at the story's beginning, you thought my boss who gave the poor performance appraisal was the main bully. However, you later learn that a less obvious bully was the one manipulating my boss. My boss displayed stereotypical bullying behaviors in the form of anger and threats. Meanwhile, the unknown bully created chaos, manipulated others, and did an excellent job of covering their tracks.

In Step One, you'll learn about the four types of workplace bullies. Two types can be found in this story, but I consider the instigator to be the covert bully who concealed their behavior. This kind of veiled bully is considered a Deceiver. For this reason, as I reference this story, I'll use the terms "Deceiver" or "workplace experience" to indicate that an event or lesson occurred in this context.

Now that you've heard both of my experiences, let's jump in. Step One is all about recognizing the signs of bullying. We'll explore why it's difficult to distinguish bullying behavior from other toxic behaviors in the workplace, the four types of workplace bullies, and the characteristics of the typical target.

Reflection Questions

Each chapter has reflection questions or activities that prompt you to apply what you are learning. This is your first opportunity to use your new knowledge.

This reflection encourages you to "try out" telling your own story. If this is the first time sharing elements of your story, this process can be a bit intimidating. If you don't feel ready to reveal your story just yet, you can return to this reflection question after you have studied more of the content.

Bonus! I've created a workbook that you can use to go a little deeper on each topic. You can access the companion workbook by scanning the QR code at the front of the book.

1) Think about my stories. Are there any similarities between my experiences and yours? If so, write down two to three parallels.

2) Next, seek out a friend or family member and share with them the essence of my story. You might say, "I just started reading this book, and the author shared her experience with a supervisor that did _____ and _____." Watch how the friend or family member reacts. Are they curious? Are they doubtful? Do they have a similar story to share? If they appear to doubt the story or seem disinterested, don't go on to the next step. Instead, try again with another friend to see if you can find a solid ally.

3) If you determine your friend or family member is open to the idea that this behavior does occur in the workplace, you might continue the conversation by saying, "I found her story intriguing because I've had a similar experience..." Then you can share one example from your encounter.

Step One – Recognizing the Signs

Are You Being Bullied at Work?

Do either of my stories from the previous chapter sound familiar? Are you being bullied at work?

Your gut may be telling you something is wrong, but your well-meaning peers see the tension between you and your co-worker as a personality conflict. Your best friend suggests you keep your head down and just do your work: "It's a good job, after all, and you are lucky to be employed." Your spouse says that you are overreacting and sound paranoid.

All this feedback, yet you know in your heart that what's happening at work—this situation between you and your co-worker (or you and your boss)—is not just a simple personality conflict. It's impossible to ignore. You don't think you are over-reacting, but the whole situation has you questioning your sanity. A thought crosses your mind, *Maybe I have become paranoid?*

How do you know you are the target of a workplace bully? The bully should be easy to spot. However, many targets, me included, don't immediately recognize they are being targeted. The first time I encountered a workplace bully, the term was not yet widely used in the United States. My grad school supervisor had what I would describe as an aggressive personality, but I believed that I had done something to deserve their criticism. For years, I was in denial that what had happened to me was bullying.

You might wonder why being able to recognize that you are being targeted is part of the solution. Well, we're all exposed

on a regular basis to some amount of negative or aggressive behavior in the workplace. However, a bully isn't just negative;
they have an agenda. That agenda is to harm you—not physically but by destroying your self-esteem, ruining your reputation, and endangering your financial stability. The quicker you
can identify that you are a target, the quicker you can take action to minimize the bully's impact.

There are many reasons bullying gets masked and therefore
overlooked. Let's discuss three of the most common.

First, over time, we've come to believe that stress, conflict, and even anger are normal parts of work. You'll hear these
themes often when people discuss work:

- Work isn't supposed to be fun.
- Work is work.
- Work is supposed to be a hard, unenjoyable, soul-sucking,
  and negative experience that we must endure to pay the
  bills and get to retirement.
- In exchange for getting paid by our employer, we must put
  up with people that we don't like and some that don't like
  us.

We've been programmed to believe that aggressive behavior
comes with the territory. We start to internalize that we just
need to *tolerate* being treated poorly at work.

This belief opens the door for bullies to target whomever
they please. Organizations infrequently put a stop to the behavior. Bullying is not against the law. The struggle that arises between bully and target is often branded as a personality conflict.
Worse yet, the target often gets labeled the problem employee,
and there are rarely consequences for the bully employee. Our
acceptance that poor workplace culture is normal conceals bullying behavior.

Second, in some organizations, competition—even to
the point of aggression—is rewarded. You only have to look
at some of the defrocked CEOs of the last twenty years to understand that organizations prefer profits over the treatment of
people. It doesn't matter *how* it gets done, just that it gets done
(and makes money). Board members and shareholders can look

the other way as long as the stock price is strong. Results can veil bad behavior.

Third, beyond workplace culture and competition, it's difficult to pinpoint bullying behavior because bullies are master manipulators. They can get you (and others around you) to believe that they have a legitimate reason for being angry with you, humiliating you, or demoting you. When you start to hear that you are incompetent, replaceable, or at fault, you may not believe it at first. But after hearing it repeatedly (especially from a supervisor), you start to believe those words. Bullies can get you to doubt the value of your contributions, your intelligence, your self-worth, even your own sanity. In essence, you start to blame yourself for their maltreatment, pushing aside or concealing the truth about their behavior.

Lending further credence to their bad behavior is the reality that many bullies can elicit help or support from coworkers. Some coworkers may comply or join in simply because they don't want to be the next target. It becomes a matter of self-preservation for your coworkers. At the very least, bullies intimidate other employees into not coming to your defense. The fact that others are condoning (or supporting) the behavior further convinces you that you are deserving of the ill-treatment.

The Challenge and the True Struggle

Even when you know these common reasons that bullying is overlooked, it can still be difficult to detect when you are being targeted. Much of bully behavior is covert; they work behind the scenes to manipulate others. A common tactic is engaging in a preemptive strike. An example of this type of attack involves the bully convincing your supervisor that you are having performance issues. The supervisor then uses their authority to deal with your performance issue even if they personally saw no such changes in your performance. Likewise, more than one human resources (HR) professional has unwittingly (or sometimes willingly) become a pawn in the bully's strategy. The bully may go to HR and say *you* are targeting *them*. Or a bully supervisor may go to HR to seek advice about their "problem employee" (you), and soon you find yourself on the wrong side of an HR investigation. This sounds like an unusual scenario, but this happens more often than you think.

When you are called incompetent, witness others joining in to support the bully, and begin to doubt your own sense of reality, it's difficult to decipher whether you are being bullied or struggling to be a competent professional. Your confusion, along with no one standing up to the bully, will leave you disoriented, emotionally drained, and struggling to hold your career together.

Experiencing workplace bullying is never your fault. You did not choose to be the target. Someone chose to specifically target you. However, you have more power in the situation than you believe. As we go further into Step One, you'll learn how to identify bully types along with behaviors and patterns that are considered bullying. The quicker you recognize the circumstances, the better you will fare emotionally and professionally. Let's begin.

The Definition of Workplace Bullying

Much of workplace bullying gets explained away as two colleagues who just can't get along. Anyone can get stressed at work or have a bad day. And every workgroup has disagreements. One outburst that's out of character for your coworker doesn't mean there is a bully in your midst. Many employees (and HR professionals) don't understand that *bullying* is a distinct set of behaviors that becomes bullying based on the behaviors' intensity, frequency, and duration.[1]

Intensity is defined as an extreme degree of strength, force, energy, or feeling. When thinking about bullying behavior in terms of intensity, consider the amount of time and energy the bully is focused on you and your behavior. Does there appear to be a constant escalating mix of behaviors that the bully uses to target you? Here are some questions to ponder to determine whether you're a bully's target:

• Does the bully demonstrate forcefulness and control by humiliating or embarrassing you in front of others?

---

1   Patricia A. Meglich, Robert H. Faley, and Cathy L. Z. DuBois, "The Influence of Actions and Actors on the Perceived Severity of Workplace Bullying," *Journal of Management Policy & Practice* 13, no. 1 (2012): 11–25.

- Do they expend a significant amount of emotional or physical energy toward you (for example, yelling at you)?
- Do they often utilize any formal power they have over you (i.e., as your supervisor) to discredit your work or threaten your job for no apparent reason?

A bully expends an exorbitant amount of time, energy, emotion, and power. This is one of the reasons workplace bullying feels distinctly different from a common conflict.

When you consider *frequency* of behavior, think about how often it occurs. Each bully will use their own unique set of tactics to establish their pattern. In the next section, we'll discuss the types of bullies, but in my experience, bullies are often more than one type. They may use a variety of approaches based on their prior success, or how *you* as the target react. Below are some typical actions a bully will utilize; note that this is not an exhaustive list:

- Intentionally excluding you from meetings
- Spreading gossip, rumors, lies, or false allegations about you
- Discrediting or humiliating you in front of others
- Providing you with unfair or excessive criticism (or a false performance review)
- Verbally abusing, attacking, or intimidating you
- Taking responsibilities away from you for no apparent reason or without explanation
- Intentionally undermining or sabotaging your work
- Dismissing or downplaying your contributions
- Displaying a pattern of repeated negative nonverbals (eye-rolling, sighing, etc.) while you are talking or sharing ideas
- Excessively monitoring or redoing your work
- Withholding information, resources, or training needed to complete your job successfully

- Repeatedly refusing requests for earned time off without explanation or reason[2]

For many of these behaviors, if you experienced them occasionally in your workplace, you wouldn't consider the actor to be a bully. When you pull together multiple behaviors in a pattern and experience them frequently, they move into bullying territory. Consider how often you experience any of the above behaviors. Do you experience them daily or weekly? If so, that's probably enough to call the behavior pattern bullying.

The final condition that defines bullying is *duration*. How long have these practices been going on? Some researchers suggest that to be defined as bullying, behaviors need to be experienced for six months or more. But if you're experiencing these tactics multiple times a week or daily, you will know long before six months that you are being targeted. Delaying six months to wait and see if the bully will stop the behavior on their own will cause psychological (and perhaps professional) damage to you.

The Four Bully Types

Personally, I struggle with the term workplace "bully." It's not because I don't think it is an accurate descriptor of the perpetrator's actions, but rather because I think it suggests a very narrow and specific type of behavior. The word bully conjures up images of the classic playground bully known for pushing, taunting, and name-calling. While this kind of overt aggressive behavior can occur in the workplace, a majority of bullying and abuse is much more subtle.

The Workplace Bullying Institute (WBI) has been conducting research and advocating for anti-bullying legislation for nearly twenty-five years. Drs. Ruth and Gary Namie founded WBI in 1997 after Ruth's experience with a bully supervisor. They introduced the term "workplace bullying" to the US in 1998.[3] Since its founding, WBI has conducted five national

---

2   Vince Scopelliti, "22 Types of Workplace Bullying Behaviour," *HR Daily Community* (blog), November 21, 2018.

3   Gary Namie, "Workplace Bullying: Escalated Incivility," *Ivey Business Journal*, (November–December 2003): 1–6.

workplace bullying surveys and dozens of online polls to understand why bullies bully, how targets are impacted, and ways bullying can be prevented.[4] Much of the data I share with you is based on WBI research.

WBI has defined four common types of workplace aggressors: Screaming Mimi, Constant Critic, Two-Headed Snake, and Gatekeeper.[5] For ease of reading, I am going to refer to the four types as the Screamer, the Critic, the Deceiver, and the Gatekeeper. While a bully may have a common method of operation and yours might fit neatly into one of these categories, know they can be a blend of types.

The Screamer

The Screamer is the stereotypical bully who is overly aggressive, angry, and demonstrates their opinions and feelings *loudly*. The WBI describes the Screamer as someone who enjoys humiliating others in a very public manner. Although the degradation and humiliation are aimed at one person, they have complete control of everyone around them. Witnesses won't defend the target or confront the bully for fear of being the next target. Through yelling, rants, and public threats, the Screamer can hold entire departments (or organizations) under their control. Ironically, WBI reports that this type of overt bullying is the rarest of the bully types.

Sample Screamer behaviors include:

- Intimidating verbally, in the form of shouting, insulting language, and sarcastic comments
- Demonstrating contempt for your contributions with repeated negative nonverbals (e.g., dramatic eye-rolling, loud sighs, scoffing)
- Intimidating physically, in the form of finger-pointing, getting in your personal space, blocking your exit from a

---

4   Workplace Bullying Institute (website), accessed October 14, 2021, https://workplacebullying.org/research/.

5   Gary Namie and Ruth Namie, *Bully at Work: What You Can Do to Stop the Hurt and Reclaim Your Dignity on the Job* (Naperville, IL: Sourcebooks, 2009).

room, or actual physical contact like shoving, "bumping" into you, or threatening with physical violence

The Critic

The Critic doesn't need the stage of the Screamer to inflict damage to the target. The Critic knows they can undermine the best of employees by discrediting their performance. The statements made by this bully go beyond constructive criticism. Comments are not intended to help you improve as a professional. In fact, the Critic is overly critical, and nothing is ever right or good enough for them. The Critic may give you an unfair or inaccurate performance appraisal or constantly hold up your mistakes as proof that you are incompetent.

Example Critic behaviors include:

- Disregarding or downplaying the significance of your contributions or your accomplishments
- Questioning your skills or qualifications
- Removing responsibilities or your title for no reason or without explanation
- Suggesting you resign

The Deceiver

The Deceiver is the most difficult to detect. Deceivers appear friendly, cooperative, and collegial to your face, but behind your back, they spread rumors and tell others about your "incompetence." They are masters at making the right connections and alliances. They know how to gain others' confidence and play colleagues against each other. When trouble erupts in the workplace due to their manipulation, these bullies have been careful to cover their tracks. Rarely does the trail lead back to the Deceiver. Targets of this type of bully often have no idea someone is undermining them until it is too late.

Deceiver behaviors to watch for include:

- Spreading rumors or gossip about you or others
- Making false accusations or allegations
- Sabotaging your work or reputation intentionally
- Using confidential information against you or others

The Gatekeeper

The Gatekeeper differs a bit from the other types of bullies. Like the Deceiver, the Gatekeeper's activities are subtle and often aren't seen by anyone but the target. Gatekeepers keep you from being successful by withholding resources like time, training, and information.

Some of the Gatekeeper's favorite tactics are:

- Excluding you from meetings
- Withholding training or information needed to do your job
- Pairing unrealistic workloads with impossible deadlines (consistently)
- Refusing to approve or allow time off without giving a reason

I don't believe these types are mutually exclusive. You can experience a Screamer who is also a Critic. A Critic could also display elements of a Gatekeeper. Between my two experiences, I have faced conduct that can be attributed to all four types of aggressors. What type of bully are you dealing with? What combinations of behaviors are you experiencing? By understanding the bully types, you can quickly identify troubling behaviors and have more success in protecting yourself.

The Prevalence of Workplace Bullying

So, how prevalent is workplace bullying? Is it a rare occurrence?

Unfortunately, the answer is no. According to a study done in January of 2021 by the WBI, 49% of the respondents had been either the target of or witnessed abusive behavior in the workplace.[6] Additional research indicates that witnessing a colleague's abuse can be just as damaging as experiencing it yourself.[7] The 2021 study results were extrapolated to estimate the prevalence of workplace bullying in the US. Potentially, 48 million US employees are, or have, experienced bullying directly. If you include witnesses to bullying, a total of 79 million US employees could be subjected to bullying on an annual basis.[8]

The Target

Some early theories about workplace bullies and their targets were developed based on childhood bully research. A popular belief has emerged that the target's characteristics made them more susceptible to bullying. Perhaps targets were "attracting" the bullying behavior by being a loner or by being more vulnerable in some way.

As further confirmation of this theory, researchers pointed to findings that those who were bullied as children often find themselves bullied as adults. Some targets of bullying find themselves being targeted additional times in different workplaces. This was true in my case. I was bullied as a child, and again targeted in two different workplaces years apart. Does this mean that I am somehow responsible for being targeted? No. WBI research also shows that one-third of targets have no history of being bullied before they are targeted in the workplace.[9]

---

6   Gary Namie, 2021 WBI U.S. Workplace Bullying Survey (Report No. 5), (Workplace Bullying Institute, 2021), https://workplacebullying.org/wp-content/uploads/2021/04/2021-Full-Report.pdf.

7   Marjan Houshmand, Jane O'Reilly, Sandra Robinson, and Angela Wolff, "Escaping Bullying: The Simultaneous Impact of Individual and Unit-level Bullying on Turnover Intentions," *Human Relations* 65, no. 7 (2012).

8   Namie, *2021 WBI U.S. Workplace Bullying Survey (Report No. 5)*.

9   Gary Namie, Workplace Bullying and Prior Experiences with Abuse (Report No. 2011-F), (Workplace Bullying Institute, 2011), https://workplacebullying.org/download/workplace-bullying-and-prior-experiences-with-abuse/?wpdmdl=2641&refresh=614685fb2e06011632011771.

So, what causes some people to be targeted more than others? In 2014, WBI conducted a poll asking respondents about characteristics they would use to describe the target. Some of the positive and desirable personality characteristics mentioned included kindness, altruism, and agreeableness. The less desirable traits included vulnerable, aggressive, and not likely (or unable) to defend themselves. Respondents included both targets and witnesses. They were asked, "Which interpersonal style best describes the person TARGETED for abusive mistreatment in bullying situations you have known?" Here were the results:

- 38% of respondents said "kind, giving, and altruistic."
- 23% described the targets as agreeable.
- 22% said they were not likely to defend themselves.
- Only 11% said that they would describe the target as vulnerable.
- Only 5% said they would describe the target as aggressive.[10]

Based on this research, it appears that being kind and agreeable are more likely factors in becoming a target than being vulnerable.

When we look at target attributes in terms of gender, the latest research from WBI indicates males and females are targeted about equally with males being targeted 51% of the time and females targeted 49% of the time. This same research reveals that males are more likely to be the aggressor (67% of the time). Women who bully most often target another woman. Bullying occurs between same gendered pairs about 60% of the time.[11] Gender may play a role when it comes to who targets whom but doesn't appear to make a difference to the target profile.

Another WBI survey from 2013 focused on the age of targets. The average age of those targeted was 42. Those under 30

---

10   Gary Namie, Personal Attributes of Bullied Targets at Work (Report No. 2014-A), (Workplace Bullying Institute, 2014), https://workplacebullying.org/download/personal-attributes-of-bullied-targets-at-work/?wpdmdl=2676&refresh=614685fb2274a1632011771.

11   Namie, *2021 WBI U.S. Workplace Bullying Survey (Report No. 5).*

were targeted only 21% of the time. The majority of targets, 75%, were 30 to 59.[12]

It could be argued that the longer you are in the workforce, the more likely you are to encounter a bully and that would account for the age of the average target. The other factor that must be considered is the fact that the further into your career you are, the more experienced, accomplished, and professional you become. Being bullied is not something that comes to the inexperienced employee often.

So why do bullies bully? I'm not sure that anyone has been able to pinpoint the exact reason. After all, workplace bullies aren't exactly lining up to be analyzed. There are some interesting theories though. Based on the target profile, we can assume that some bullies engage because they are jealous of the more accomplished, experienced, and influential person. One WBI survey revealed that 34.5% of individuals were targeted because the bully felt threatened by either the target's superior technical skills or their personal popularity among colleagues.[13]

An experienced professional has a lot to lose and far to fall. They also won't see it coming. The bully may derive pleasure in the suffering that goes along with unraveling someone's career. Or perhaps the bully feels the need to knock them down (or out) to look good. On the other hand, the reason may be simple and practical—the bully wants the target's position.

Another theory is that the bully targets someone to create a distraction from their own incompetence, lack of work ethic, or integrity. If bullies can keep others focused on someone else's behavior, maybe no one will notice them leaving early, gossiping, or goofing off during work. Or the bully senses that the target may have the moral fortitude to stand up to them or turn them in for compliance or integrity infractions.

---

12 Gary Namie, Age of Workplace Bullied Targets (Report No. 2013-G), (Workplace Bullying Institute, 2013), https://workplace-bullying.org/download/age-of-workplace-bullied-targets-2/?wpdm-dl=2671&refresh=614692643c2721632014948.

13 Gary Namie, How Bullies Select Their Targets (Report No. 2012-I), (Workplace Bullying Institute, 2012), https://workpla-cebullying.org/download/how-bullies-select-their-targets/?wpdm-dl=2657&refresh=614688e5196f31632012517.

Sometimes I think bullies just enjoy the control over the chaos they create. Regardless of the reasoning, bullies are most likely not mentally healthy people. Mentally healthy people don't derive pleasure from others' pain.

The argument that you as a target have attracted this abusive situation is the same as saying that you created your abuse by being a *positive, helpful, responsible, experienced, and productive employee.* This argument does not hold a drop of water. We cannot lay the crux of the problem at the feet of the target. The blame lies squarely on the bully.

After reviewing these signs and types of bullies, you can probably confirm, without a doubt, that you are a target of a workplace bully. This realization comes with a variety of emotions. Relief that you are not losing your mind and that someone believes you. Feeling sick to your stomach because of the situation you are in. Confusion and fear about what to do next.

I encourage you to use the reflection questions to take action. Dig into the details about the behaviors you are witnessing. The greater understanding you have about the type of bully you are facing, the easier it will be to apply next steps.

As you continue taking action, you'll start to feel stronger. You'll feel more hopeful when you can see the light at the end of the tunnel. Consistently apply what you are learning, and you will be able to break free.

Reflection Questions

This set of reflection questions will help you create a bully profile and your target profile. You can use the questions below as a guide, or you can use the detailed profile builder worksheet in the companion workbook.

1) Which type(s) of bullying are you experiencing?
   • The Screamer
   • The Critic
   • The Deceiver
   • The Gatekeeper

2) What kinds of behaviors do you recognize? What are the bully's favorite tactics? (Refer to the section, "The Four Bully Types" for a list of ideas.)

3) How do you align with the typical target profile?
   - Are you between the ages of 30–59?
   - Are you an experienced professional?
   - Are you a person of influence in your company/department?
   - Do you consider yourself kind, altruistic, and/or agreeable?

4) Based on the bully's behaviors and your target profile, what is your best guess as to the bully's motivations? Are they hiding their own incompetence or something else? Do they want your position? Are they intimidated by your popularity or skills?

Step Two – Navigating the Chaos

Developing Your Bully Intelligence

During Step One, we discussed how to define workplace bullying and the types of bully personas. In this step, we'll continue to gain an understanding of how and why bullies take hold. The goal here is to build your ability to recognize bullying early.

As you learn more about how a bully operates, this knowledge becomes part of your armor. The bully will use numerous tools against you—your emotions, your good nature, your fear for your job, and potentially even a network of helpers. You need to utilize all tools available to protect yourself. By developing awareness of how a bully finds a target and the helpers they employ, you are developing your Bully Intelligence. This will serve you well in the future and may even enable you to prevent others from becoming targets.

Bullying catches so many professionals off guard. Why? Because most of us are not malicious people by nature. We learned in Step One that many targets are considered agreeable and positive professionals. We are too busy doing our jobs well to have time to consider bullying someone for our own gain. This is exactly why we struggle to believe the chaos is real.

We need our Bully Intelligence to look at the situation more critically than we normally would. As responsible and mature professionals, we're more likely to give someone the benefit of the doubt. We can easily dismiss the confusion, miscommunication, or comments as someone having a bad day. We give people another chance because we suspect something in their personal life is impacting their stress level. But we need to stop providing luxurious latitude to people consistently and maliciously misbehaving in the workplace. Our Bully Intelligence can provide us with a foundation for detecting and identifying an aggressor before they can do too much damage.

A key aspect of Bully Intelligence is understanding how targeting occurs. For most targets, the attack from the aggressor appears out of nowhere, but I contend that the bully lays groundwork as they plan their assault. Four stages occurred in both my incidents. Let's learn the process the bully goes through from initially selecting a target to damaging the target's career.

Understanding the Stages of Targeting

In both of my experiences, there are four clear stages of targeting. Aggressors are selective with their targets. Note, though, that with a bully running a long-game deception, it may feel abrupt when their intentions are suddenly made visible to you. Most often the target and bully are new to the working relationship. Either the bully is new in the position, or you are new to the workgroup. There are four escalating stages of targeting:

1) The bully sizes up/identifies the target.
2) The bully limits the target's ability to do their best work.
3) The bully destroys the target's professional reputation.
4) The bully takes the target out of their position.

Let's explore each stage.

In stage one, the bully sizes up the target. The bully watches, then tests the waters. The goal of stage one is to see who a good target might be. The bully might ask themselves questions like:

• Who has the farthest to fall?
• Whose job might I want?
• Who is the most agreeable?
• Who is the most dedicated?
• Who is the team's go-to person?

- Who won't gossip with me?
- Who won't fight back?
- Who is the most talented?
- Who can I get to trust me the most?

Depending on your bully's goal, what they are watching for may vary. If the bully is new to the workplace, they may also assess the culture. Bullying cannot exist in a vacuum. If the environment is conducive to getting away with the behavior, the bully will take advantage of the lack of accountability.

I remember one specific, seemingly mundane incident with my grad school supervisor that should have been lost by now but remains vivid in my memory twenty-five years later. During one of the first weeks in my position as a research assistant, I volunteered to call a researcher who had created a survey that we wanted to use in our research. The call was long distance, so I needed to make the call from my supervisor's phone. While the supervisor observed, I made the call. I ended up leaving a message. When I hung up, my supervisor said, "You did a really nice job leaving that message. It was very professional."

On the surface, you might think this was just a supervisor giving positive feedback to their new employee. The problem wasn't what they said, but how. It was said with an undertone of wonderment mixed with skepticism, as if I couldn't possibly be capable of such professionalism. They didn't smile at me when giving the compliment. Instead, they just looked at me through squinted eyes.

I responded, "Thank you. I did things like this all the time as an undergrad."

But they just kept staring at me and murmured, "Hmmm."

It was such an odd interaction that it stuck in my mind. As I look back, I wonder whether that was the moment that my bully supervisor had chosen their target. I can't be sure. The interaction had made me a little uneasy but certainly didn't raise any red flags on what was to come.

My supervisor had been derogatory and negative with our team from day one, but it was after this interaction that my supervisor started aiming comments directly at me. I would argue that the constant berating of the team's efforts was an attempt to keep the entire team a little off-kilter. By making little digs or comments, my supervisor could observe people's reactions. Someone who didn't react to them or spoke against the supervisor probably wouldn't be a good target. The bully could watch and take note of anyone that seemed rattled by their comments.

Besides being a helpful, agreeable, and responsible employee (all of the research assistants fit that description), I had the smallest support system. I was entirely new to the college and the community, and I didn't have any family nearby. Most of my fellow students had either been at the university for undergrad or lived with other family members. I had never experienced someone in a professional capacity speaking to me like my supervisor did. I will admit that it did rattle me. I was probably visibly upset by my supervisor's comments.

In the second stage, the bully wants to limit your ability to do your best work. This means ramping up the fear, the insults, and/or the pressure to the point that you are so focused on protecting yourself from their attack that you can't possibly be successful. In this stage, they are trying to destroy you from within.

Your reactions and emotions in response to being bullied can inadvertently bolster the effectiveness of the bully. As you become more anxious and fearful of your aggressor, going to work each day becomes more and more difficult. The situation may become traumatic at this stage. The bully has set you up perfectly to experience a self-fulfilling prophecy. The bully tells you that you are a *bad employee,* then you turn into a *bad employee.*

When responsible, professional adults suddenly find their work, their reputation, and their ability to make a living under assault, performance inevitably suffers. We can become hypervigilant when it comes to completing our work accurately. This slows us down and reduces the amount of work we were once able to easily accomplish. We might become so anxious or nervous around the bully that we start to make mistakes. Or, under pressure from impossible deadlines, we may become so rushed that we make a mistake. Similarly, we can become so afraid of the consequences of making a mistake that we may use poor judgment and cover it up. The distraction is so complete that the overall quality of our work suffers.

As an experienced professional, you know when you are

doing good work and when you are not. You can feel yourself making mistakes and struggling to do the level and quality of work that is up to your own personal standards. When you start to believe the bully's rhetoric, the bully has seeped into your head. Despite years of success and glowing reviews, suddenly you feel like a failure. The bully is systematically eroding your confidence and your self-esteem.

Within this second stage of targeting, others start to notice you unravel. Suddenly you *are* making mistakes, coming in late, calling in sick, or missing deadlines. Others become aware of this drop in performance. They don't see the same performance slip from the bully. Your errors then become further proof for the bully that their judgment and treatment of you is justified. Your bully uses your errors to build a case against you in full view of your other colleagues, leader, or HR department.

The ability for the bully to use you against yourself is perhaps the most insidious thing about workplace bullying. What's worse is that long after you have left this workplace and the bully behind, those doubts about yourself and your talent can persist for years.

In some cases, stages two and three can overlap, but in either case, stage two is the pivotal stage for putting a pin in you professionally at this workplace. Stage three is about destroying your professional reputation. Bullies will talk to others about your performance. They will try to get others to see it their way. They may preemptively go to HR to ask for advice about their "problem employee." They may ruin your reputation with leaders in other departments, lest you try to transfer to another area of the company or enlist help from former colleagues. They may go to HR or a coworker to "ask for advice," when in reality, they are looking for another opportunity to share examples of your troubled performance. In the ultimate unprofessional act, they may speak to other members of your team about your performance. Yet rarely is the bully caught in such behaviors. At this point, many people have already seen the proof of your slipping performance with their own eyes.

Stage four is game, set, match. This stage is about taking you out of your position or the workplace completely. If you reach this stage, you have already endured a tremendous amount of abuse.

You may decide to preemptively jump to this stage by making the decision to leave your workplace and the abuse behind. I know this is not a decision to take lightly, and we'll discuss more about navigating that decision during Step Five.

Another outcome that could occur at this stage is you are demoted or fired. Both are the ultimate humiliation for the responsible, experienced professional. The WBI found that approximately 12% of targets were fired. In comparison, only 9% of bullies were terminated.[14] The toll on a target's career path is significant. WBI found that 67% of targets end up losing or leaving a job they love because of a workplace bully.[15]

You might say at this point, "Dawn, if I leave, aren't I just giving the bully what they want?"

Yes and no. The bully enjoys the process even more than the outcome. My grad school supervisor had done this same act to students before me, and I have *no* doubt that they continued this pattern after me. Recently, friends encouraged me to Google my grad school supervisor. Lo and behold as late as 2016, they were in that same position. I am sure there is an entire club of us who were targeted by this same person from at least the mid-1990s on.

By leaving a job, you aren't condoning what the bully is doing. But by recognizing it, refusing the long-term abuse, and getting out, you are protecting your career, reputation, and sanity. You are also saving yourself the heartache of being demoted or fired.

Uncovering the Signs of the Deceiver

You'll recall from my workplace story that on the surface, my boss seemingly went from supportive colleague to bully overnight. My boss's actions align with a Critic bully type. They provided an unfair (and surprise) review with no real data to support their opinion. They removed some of my responsibilities without explanation. They disregarded any positive contri-

14   Namie, *2021 WBI U.S. Workplace Bullying Survey (Report No. 5).*

15   Namie, *2021 WBI U.S. Workplace Bullying Survey (Report No. 5).*

butions I'd made to the organization and threatened demotion. Classic Critic! Their conduct certainly did damage to me, but I don't believe they would have carried out those acts without the covert bully manipulating their perception of me.

The covert bully was a Deceiver. They were nice to my face while spreading rumors about me behind my back. They made false allegations about my performance. They intentionally sabotaged my reputation. All classic Deceiver tactics. Such stealthy activity warrants unpacking so you'll be able to identify the Deceiver before it's too late.

Often, the Deceiver is nearly impossible to detect. Their behaviors are often not visible until the fourth stage of targeting when your reputation is ruined and your work has declined. After reflecting on my experience, I recognize signs that I believe can help someone identify a Deceiver earlier in the targeting process. The behaviors I'm about to share may not be typical of all Deceiver bullies, but hopefully you'll get a sense of some behaviors to watch for.

When it came to my attention that someone was manipulating my boss's perception of me, I thought about all of my co-workers. None of them had outwardly expressed an issue with me, or at least, not an issue that would lead to this behavior.

However, there was *someone* in the office who was often gossiping about others. There was *someone* who was frequently disparaging the work of other colleagues. There was *someone* who was pervasively negative about the organization and the decisions of leadership. This *someone* was telling me about these things under the guise that I hold their confidence. In fact, they said that I was the *only one* they trusted with these "concerns" and that they were only "venting" to me because they trusted me. They counted on my good nature. They knew I would listen. They took advantage of my professionalism to ensure that I wouldn't reveal anything they told me.

As I began to focus on this person as a potential culprit, I began to realize how often the Deceiver would share controversial pieces of information with a group of employees who would then get riled up. The Deceiver would conveniently step back from the conversation, not participating but taking it all in. I also recognized how often they would dig for information in a conversation. They'd say, "So-and-so said this . . . what do you think about that?" Or sometimes it was "This was discussed at the board meeting. What are your thoughts?" People trusted this person. I trusted them. We trusted them because they trusted us. But the Deceiver was not worthy of our trust.

As their behavior became more visible (at least to me), I began to catch the Deceiver's small slips. For example, a colleague might share a concern about something the Deceiver had said. I would realize that I had heard that same information from the bully in one of our "confidential" sessions. I began to realize that the Deceiver was probably having these "confidential" sessions with most if not all of my colleagues. The bully was often sharing the same info, but each person thought they were the only one who knew.

In hindsight, this Deceiver did not waste time creating chaos. Starting the second week they were employed, they started attempts to undermine my confidence in my colleagues. I have no doubt that the Deceiver was doing the same with my fellow coworkers and their supervisors.

The Deceiver started in immediately on our marketing person: "What a poor job they did . . . they didn't really know how to market . . . anyone could create better materials than they did." The marketing employee didn't last long after the bully's arrival; they were let go within the year.

Then the bully started in on the marketing assistant: "They arrived late on Monday mornings. They must have a drinking problem, right?" The marketing assistant was eventually let go too. Then it was an office assistant, then another director. . . . You can see the pattern.

I should have known that anyone gossiping *to me* was probably also gossiping *about me*. The most puzzling fact is that leaders acted on the Deceiver's information without investigating. The Deceiver was able to garner so much trust from others that the bully was able to manipulate multiple leaders to demote or fire their employees based on the Deceiver's information. It sounds crazy. It sounds paranoid. It's not. It happened. It could be happening in your workplace right now.

To continue building your Bully Intelligence, take note of these behaviors that may be early signals there is a Deceiver in your midst:

- Gossiping
- Digging for information
- Complaining incessantly to you in private, but being the picture of positivity with others
- Asking you to keep confidences or secrets for them
- Managing up (mistreating peers or subordinates, but being charming and professional to leaders or others with influence over their career)

This isn't an exhaustive list, but pay particular attention to anyone who appears to have two sides to their personality or displays different types of behavior based on who they're with. Even if they do not turn out to be a bully, manipulating their image is a sure sign of trouble. Steer clear.

Exposing the Bully's Network

The Deceiver is an excellent example of how a bully leverages their network. Building on what we know about the Deceiver's tactics, let's move into a discussion about the bully's network. I contend that workplace bullying cannot occur without a support system. The Deceiver would not have been successful without people to manipulate. Behind every bully, you'll find a network of people who ignore, enable, or even participate in the conduct. In my workplace experience, the helper (my boss) became a bully too. The next section explores the people, who by action (or inaction), continue the cycle of bullying.

Helpers

Helpers play an active role in continuing the bully's mission to annihilate your confidence, reputation, and career. Sometimes helpers know and understand what they are doing, and other times they are an ignorant pawn in the bully's game. Helpers can be in the form of company leaders, fellow coworkers, and even HR professionals. You may have even found yourself an unwitting accomplice to a bully.

Often, the activity the bully asks the naive helper to do is framed as an effort to improve the team or to assist in identifying training or quality gaps. For example, a helper may be asked to report on any mistakes witnessed from one particular colleague. Taking the activity one step further, a helper might be asked to monitor the activities of a particular colleague and report back on items like arrival or departure time, time spent on breaks, time spent in conversation, or what's said in collegial conversations. In more extreme cases, helpers may use their network (inside or outside the workplace) to dig up info that may be used against the target.

Helpers also further the bully's agenda by acting on false accusations or misinformation. A bully might not have formal authority over the person being targeted but may strategically feed information to someone that is in formal power, such as a supervisor or HR employee. If the supervisor or HR employee takes the information at face value, it can do great harm to the target.

When my situation with my grad school supervisor reached a tipping point, I requested a meeting with my supervisor and their leader. In that meeting, I explained what was happening from my perspective and expressed that I wasn't being treated with the respect that should be attributed to a responsible adult. My supervisor responded by yelling and pointing in my face, "I am older than you. I am smarter than you. I have more education than you. *You* are *not* my equal."

The bully's supervisor simply listened. At the end of the conversation, the supervisor's leader asked me to consider whether I could continue in my assistantship under the current circumstances. I was to call my supervisor's leader by the end of the next day to let them know my decision.

When I called the next day, I stated that the behavior displayed in the meeting should have given them a glimpse of what I had been dealing with. I conveyed how sorry I was that I could not continue in my assistantship. I explained that I wasn't one to give up easily. I would not have given in to the situation had it not escalated to this point. I wasn't a quitter.

The leader responded, "That is exactly what you are—a quitter. You need to work a nine-to-five job where you don't have to think. You are going to have a very tough time in your career after you leave here." I was stunned by the response. I wondered why the leader had turned against me. I'd had very little interaction with them since arriving on campus. I knew they'd not seen enough of my performance to decide on their own. *Why would the leader continue protecting someone who had clearly done this before? Didn't they wonder why students dropped out of the program each year?*

Knowing what I know now, I realize one of two things were going on (or maybe both). One, my supervisor was telling their leader about me, the "problem" employee, all along. Since the leader had no reason not to believe their employee (and research partner) of many years, they assumed that those who left the program did so because they couldn't "cut it." The leader had no idea my supervisor was systematically driving us out.

The second reason the leader might have had for protecting their direct report was money. I am assuming that the research project I was working on brought a significant amount of money into the university. The leader couldn't risk the program receiving any negative press or scrutiny because the grant funding could be cut or lost completely. Also, they both planned to publish based on the research being done. Promotions, additional funding, and potentially tenure were dependent on the research being completed successfully.

I left my assistantship shortly after this conversation, and I left school less than two months later at the end of the semester. I can't be sure if my supervisor's boss knew what was going on or was being manipulated. Either way, the leader played the crucial role of a helper who continued the abuse.

HR as a Helper

Time and time again, I've heard reports of targets seeking help from their company's HR department, and almost every story ends with "it just got worse." Having worked in an HR department for a good chunk of my career, I've formulated a few theories about why this might be the case.

First, I don't think HR employees are trained to recognize and handle bullying. Bullying isn't like harassment or discrimination. There is no law against bullying in the US. Additionally, the variety of behaviors and bully personas we discussed during Step One can make it difficult to determine a clear pattern.

Second, depending on the relationship the bully has with HR, the investigator may be more inclined to believe the bully. This can occur with either a supervisor bully or a peer bully. Before you even realize what's going on, the bully may have already contacted HR about you as a problem performer in a preemptive strike. By the time you come to report the abusive behavior, an opinion about you and your performance has already been formed.

The HR department still may investigate the situation, but just like any investigation, they will eventually have to interview the person accused of bullying. By notifying the aggressor that there has been a report, the attention may trigger an escalation of the behavior. If the aggressor genuinely didn't understand the negative impact of their behavior, the report to HR would trigger an immediate behavior change. However, the goal of the bully is to *intentionally* inflict harm. The bully won't just reverse the behavior because they are told to stop. While you would like to think that the HR department is a good place to get assistance, depending on the staff's experience and familiarity with the bullying phenomenon, you may not get a tremendous amount of help. Proceed with caution.

I have spent more than a decade working in HR. I know my HR friends and colleagues work hard to create safe spaces for employees; yet there are too many examples of bullying targets finding themselves on the wrong side of an HR investigation or alone in an escalating situation. The best thing an organization can do to combat bullying is to educate HR staff and employees about bullying behaviors. When employees in an organization have a common language to describe what is happening and employees can recognize the behaviors early, you're much more likely to be able to hold bullies accountable. When employees trust that HR understands the impact these behaviors have on both employees and the broader organization, they are more likely to report. Bullying may not be illegal, but you do not have to tolerate it in your organization.

Bystanders

Bystanders, as indicated by their name, contribute to bullying by doing nothing. In my story about my grad school supervisor, you may remember that there were two fellow students that came to me and expressed their knowledge of and sympathy for my plight. Based on their own situations, they were unwilling or unable to step forward and stand with me against our supervisor. They both had a lot to lose in terms of their careers and reputations.

I am grateful for their willingness to be a silent ally and call *my* attention to a long-standing and pervasive pattern by the supervisor. I don't blame them for their inaction. Knowing that they recognized the issue didn't make it any less painful to stand alone against my aggressive supervisor. Unfortunately, their unwillingness to act allowed the supervisor to go on tormenting a new student each year.

Bystanders enable bullies with their inaction. By doing nothing, they are still "helping" the bully. Well-developed Bully Intelligence includes understanding and recognizing the active and passive roles played by both helper and bystander. Here are a few questions to ask yourself to avoid being surprised by a helper.

- Has a close colleague *suddenly* distanced from you? This could be a number of things, but in the context of active bullying, it can mean they are trying to avoid being the next target by keeping their distance. Alternatively, someone could be turning them away from you.
- Has a colleague *suddenly* taken a keen interest in your work schedule or process? They may ask in casual conversation, "Busy morning! What time did you get in?" Or they want to know how you do a particular process in painstaking detail.
- Has a colleague *suddenly* become interested in your opinions on other employees, leadership, or the company in general?

In addition to watching for sudden behavior changes in their coworkers, I also advise targets to share personal information or opinions cautiously around new colleagues they don't know well.

Proceeding with Caution

You might be concerned that you will become hypervigilant, looking for bullies and their helpers around every corner. I believe it's worthwhile to build up a healthy dose of caution. Look for the behaviors and the patterns. If you can recognize the behaviors in targeting stages one or two, you'll at the very least minimize the damage done to your career.

By recognizing the signs, understanding the stages, and being aware of the network of helpers, you're well on your way to developing your Bully Intelligence. You'll be better prepared to protect yourself (or someone else) in the future.

Reflection Questions

Work through the first four reflection questions below to help you formalize your Bully Intelligence. (You can see a full list of Bully Intelligence attributes in the companion workbook.) The final two reflection questions will help you identify where you need to protect or improve your level of performance. Remember that your slipping performance can support the bully's lies and is the key to stage two of targeting being successful. Questions four and five will help you identify how you can do everything you can to maintain your level of performance under the circumstances.

1) What stage of targeting are you in?

   Stage 1: The bully is aggressive but may not have selected a specific target yet.

   Stage 2: The bully is preventing you from doing your best work (e.g., by intimidation, withholding resources, verbally cutting you down, etc.). Your performance has begun to suffer, and people have started to notice.

   Stage 3: The bully is going after your professional reputation and pointing out your performance to others.

   Stage 4: The bully is ramping up efforts to get you demoted or fired (or to get you to leave).

2) What signs or behaviors do you see that tells you what stage you are in?

3) What helpers exist? What types of "help" do you suspect they are providing?

4) If you are in stage two (or later), has your performance started to slip? If so, in what ways?

5) What steps can you take to shore up your performance? Some examples might include working physically farther from the bully to limit distractions or double-checking your work to limit the possibility of an error.

Step Three – Containing Emotions

Preventing the Bully from Using YOU Against YOU

During Step Two, we learned the importance of building your Bully Intelligence. Perhaps you are reading this book because you are knee-deep in your bullying situation. You probably wish that you'd known how to spot a bully much earlier in your career. At this point, you may feel powerless, but I am here to tell you that you have more power than you think. Steps Three, Four, and Five focus on actions you can take now to minimize damage while you move yourself away from the aggressor.

Step Three centers on emotions. If you've experienced workplace bullying, you know the dizzying array of emotions that occur throughout the experience—you may feel shock, anger, confusion, sadness, and fear, just to name a few. Workplace bullying is personal. Every emotion you feel is justified; however, your emotions can also fan the flames the bully has lit.

Part of the bully's strategy is to target your emotions. Remember when your mother told you that the bully on the playground was just trying to get a rise out of you? Bullies count on you reacting emotionally. In fact, they may get some deep pleasure from witnessing your emotional pain or soaking in the emotional chaos they have caused. But workplace bullies won't stop there—they'll exploit your reaction.

We mustn't let our emotions perpetuate the abuse. Don't let your emotions betray you. There's nothing wrong with feeling the emotions associated with the situation. Understand, though, how bullies leverage your own emotions against you, so you can fight to neutralize your emotions as best you can.

After my distressing performance review, the person that I would eventually learn had orchestrated my demise (the Deceiver) was constantly pushing me to reveal what was going on. The Deceiver commented, "You don't seem very happy lately. What's wrong?"

I didn't know at the time that they were the one pulling my boss's strings. Lucky for me, I didn't reveal anything to the Deceiver. I didn't say anything to anyone about my performance review. I was embarrassed. I stayed focused on my work and didn't talk to colleagues much. If someone asked why I wasn't being social, I would just say I was busy. When the Deceiver asked me directly about my visibly strained relationship with my boss, I simply said, "We just don't have a need to communicate much right now."

I shudder now to think that I could have confided in the Deceiver. I trusted them. We talked often during the day. We had even attended outings together. They were digging because they wanted to see the fruits of their labor. They wanted to see me cry, get angry, and fall apart, all the while playing the role of the supportive colleague. If I would have revealed anything, they could have sat back and admired their deranged handiwork while I pounded more nails into my own coffin.

Once your emotions are out there in the open, bullies are experts at leveraging them against you. Remember that most workplace bullies are aiming for your reputation. Your emotions, whether they are expressed in angry words or tearful sobs, will be laid out as proof that you don't deserve to be in your position. They may suggest that you can no longer handle the pressure. Your outburst of emotion will be used as evidence against you.

Your emotions can lead your work to suffer too. When you are angry, sad, or fearful, your full attention isn't on your work. You may not be able to be as productive as you once were. You may try to avoid working with the bully, which could create inefficiencies and communication issues. You may not be sleeping well, and lack of rest prevents you from doing your best work. While you were a stellar employee a couple of months ago, the emotional toll may create an *actual* performance issue. In other words, you are handing the bully (or your boss) a legitimate reason to demote or fire you. Worse yet, your coworkers may also see you slipping, and they won't give it another thought when one day you are just gone.

Part of the joy that a bully gets from bullying is the embarrassment that you will inevitably feel. The bully counts on you feeling embarrassed so they can maintain their aggressive efforts. If you are embarrassed, you won't want others to know. You'll keep the bully's confidence. In effect, you'll be protecting the bully and allowing the bullying to continue unchecked. Your own embarrassment can become a bully's best ally.

Embarrassment coupled with your professionalism further aids the bully. Bullies often target the most professional person on the team because their level of professionalism will delay them from revealing to anyone that they are being bothered by a bully.

Here are a few of the common reasons targets say they didn't seek help earlier.

- "I didn't want to make a big deal out of it."
- "I didn't want to get anyone in trouble."
- "I am a mature, responsible professional, and I thought I could handle it."
- "I thought maybe this person was just going through a bad time, and I wanted to give them the benefit of the doubt."

Many targets have been done in by their own professionalism. In addition, targets' embarrassment limits their support system and often prevents them from getting the emotional help they need in a timely manner.

Angry yet? The way that bullies can manipulate you, and others, is maddening. Knowing that your emotion can (and probably will) be used against you is a key aspect of your Bully Intelligence. To outwit this master manipulator, you need the ability to somewhat manipulate your own emotions. I wouldn't normally advocate for someone to mask their emotions, but the key to survival is remaining as composed and professional as you can in the presence of the bully.

Mask with Emotional Labor

As you cope with the day-to-day reality of working alongside a bully, you are experiencing a host of emotions from anger and fear to sadness and frustration. You may feel anxious, nervous, or even depressed. Confusion, avoidance, and even denial may set in.

Expressing strong emotions in the workplace can be normal and productive. For example, we can passionately (yet professionally) express our opposition to an idea that we feel is wrong. We can feel sadness (and even cry) when our coworker moves on. Or we can express frustration with a coworker who repeatedly misses deadlines.

Often as a part of our jobs, it's necessary to contain our emotions to complete our work successfully. Let's use the example of a customer service representative (or service rep, for short). It would be inappropriate for a service rep to get angry at a customer who is upset about a charge on their bill. The service rep must maintain composure and withhold their own strong emotions even if the customer is using profanity or verbally attacking the service rep's intelligence. Likewise, it would be inappropriate for a lawyer to start crying in the courtroom after they lose a jury trial, even though the lawyer is devastated for the client. The concept of monitoring and containing your emotions as a job requirement is termed *emotional labor*.

Emotional labor is the reason the airplane pilot can remain calm in a crisis and why your server still greets you with a smile despite being exhausted at the end of a very long shift. We all perform some form of emotional labor every day. It's why you didn't scream at your coworker last week or roll your eyes at the last company board meeting. It isn't easy. Emotions are high, but so are the stakes. I'm confident you can perform emotional labor in a bullying situation too.

Think about emotional labor as putting on your game face. In this case, you need to put on your Olympic-level game face. No Olympic athlete would compete without practice. Visualizing your controlled response can help build your emotional labor muscles. I know when there's so much turmoil at work and you are hurting and scared, the last thing you want to do is think about how you are going to respond to the bully.

Nonetheless, being thoughtful and intentional about how you will react can prevent you from overreacting in the moment. Ask a friend to help you practice reacting calmly. Or visualize the next time you are confronted and practice taking a deep breath, walking away, or calmly responding verbally.

Outside of work, please *do* healthily express your emotions. It's not healthy to completely hide your emotions. Seek support from friends, family, and mental health professionals as needed. Step Four discusses maintaining mental health in more detail.

Disarm with Responses

If you are dealing with a bully who routinely attacks you verbally, practicing not only your emotional reaction but also your own verbal response can be advantageous. Keeping a few disarming phrases in your back pocket enables you to exit a conversation quickly. You may even find you can throw the bully off or slow down the attacks (if only for a short time).

Here are some response options. Practice saying these phrases in a calm, neutral, or positive tone. Avoid sarcasm.

- "Thank you for your thoughts. I will take those under advisement."
- "Interesting point. Thank you for sharing."
- "You really keep me on my toes. I appreciate your commitment to my development."
- "Your spirited reaction added life to what would have been an otherwise boring meeting."

Please don't take this idea in the wrong way—I am not making light of the abuse you are enduring. I want to empower you to maintain your strength as you extricate yourself from the situation.

Use the space below to create some of your own phrases. The options you come up with should not attack the bully's character, personality, or work performance. It's critical that you be able to maintain professionalism when using this technique.

Consider practicing your phrases out loud with a friend. Just like a prize fighter who practices responding to different types of punches, you'll be better prepared if you practice using your phrases in a simulated situation. State your phrases in a confident, polite, and positive tone of voice. Ask your friend for feedback on your tone and how the phrase might be interpreted by others.

_____

_____

_____

_____

_____

_____

_____

Story - Please Don't Fire Me!

With all this emphasis on emotional labor, you're probably saying, "Dawn, are you crazy? My life and career have been turned upside down. I'm not sleeping. I'm anxious and crying frequently. I am fighting for my career, my livelihood, and my sanity!"

I understand. I was not the picture of composure and neutrality in the beginning either. During my workplace experience, I distinctly remember after one time my boss came into my office and angrily took yet another project away from me, I was quite the opposite of composure. I remember crying, begging, and pleading with them, "Why are you doing this to me? Please don't fire me. I could lose my house."

They didn't answer me. I'm assuming now it's because my boss really didn't have a good answer for what they were doing.

Moments after this conversation with my boss, I was in the ladies' room cleaning myself up and one of my colleagues entered. They said, "You need to stop crying at work. It's going to get you fired." My colleagues didn't know what was happening. I was too "professional" to tarnish my boss's reputation by telling other employees what was going on. I still blamed myself for my disgraceful review, and I was too embarrassed and ashamed to tell anyone.

Thinking back now, if they had known, they would have either been shocked by my boss's sudden behavior change or they wouldn't have believed me. They didn't see my boss's behavior, and I wasn't talking about what was going on. What they did see was me completely losing it at work. If I had been fired at that point, I think most of my colleagues would have assumed that I had cracked under the pressure and had done something to deserve the loss of my job.

Anchor with Affirmations

Just days after my devastating review, I was scheduled to make a two-hour trip to another part of the state to speak to a group of potential clients. Because my boss had expressed reservations about my ability to represent the organization, I asked my boss if they still wanted me to be the one to present. Surprisingly, they did want me to go and speak.

I was still reeling from the experience of the previous week, but I was determined to hold myself together. As I hopped in the car early that morning, I happened to put in a CD of passages of Bible scripture set to song. One song was based on Philippians 4 titled, "The God of Peace Will Be with You." The chorus repeats the phrase "what is true, what is right, what is pure, think of these."[16] I found this song calmed me and gave me strength. I played it on repeat for most of the two-hour trip.

When I got to my destination, I found a room full of clients eager to hear my information. Two of my coworkers that

---

16   Mary Fielder, Netha Larsen, Rob Ondras, Blake Parker, Jennie Williamson, and Jimmie Young, "The God of Peace Will Be with You," *By Grace: Songs for the Masses Living as God's Children*, vol. 2, 2004, compact disc. Nashville, TN: Takestone Music.

were located in a different office were also in attendance. I made my presentation and received compliments and questions afterward. I considered it a successful session, and I certainly didn't feel I had "struggled" to represent the organization "well." I went to lunch with my coworkers afterward. We had a good lunch and great conversation. I said nothing about my performance review, and I didn't let out a hint of what had happened days earlier. I found myself throughout the day repeating the phrase in my head "what is true, what is right, think of these" as an affirmation. I don't think I would have been able to hold myself together that day without those soothing and strengthening words.

I later looked up the full verse that the song was based on. Quoting from Eugene Peterson's *The Message*, he translates Philippians 4 as "Summing it all up, friends, I'd say you'll do best by filling your minds and meditating on things true, noble, reputable, authentic, compelling, gracious—the best, not the worst; the beautiful, not the ugly; things to praise, not things to curse. Put into practice what you learned from me, what you heard and saw and realized. Do that, and God, who makes everything work together, will work you into his most excellent harmonies."[17]

At this point, *I did not know* that what was happening to me was based on lies. *I did not know* that someone was intentionally sabotaging my reputation. *I did not know* that someone was not being authentic and noble in their intentions. Looking back now, this was certainly a message I needed to hear to give me strength, but I had no way of knowing how prophetic this verse would become.

I knew I needed to redouble my efforts to stay strong and confident at work. I continued to listen to the song in my car. I prayed for strength. I sought out quotes that inspired me and looked at them throughout the day. I was terrified and falling apart on the inside, but I hoped that I was appearing stronger on the outside. If you are a person of faith, I encourage you to seek out a scripture that can be your affirmation. Or find any quote or affirmation that you can repeat to yourself throughout

17   Eugene H. Peterson, *The Message: The New Testament in Contemporary Language* (Colorado Springs, CO: NavPress Publishing Group, 2003).

the day to get you through. Here are some examples you can try.

- One day at a time.
- One foot in front of the other.
- This too shall pass.
- I am strong.
- Day by day I'm getting stronger.
- Heat sharpens metal.
- Truth is on my side.

Write down some phrases that you can remember and will give you strength to get through the day.

_____

_____

_____

_____

_____

_____

_____

Whatever happens, continue to be your professional self. Being professional doesn't mean that you can't defend yourself. You don't need to just stand there and accept the behavior, but you should do your best to not stoop to the bully's level or add fuel to the fire. I know this is *so* difficult. The bully's behavior is inexcusable. Advocate for yourself, calmly respond to verbal attacks, and seek help through the proper organizational channels (if you choose). Continue to do your job to the best of your ability. Strive to keep your head held high and your emotions neutral.

Reflection Questions

This set of questions will help you determine how much your emotions impact your ability to do your work and identify a few ways to maintain your emotions in the face of your aggressor. Question three requires a partner to help you practice the disarming responses technique.

1) What emotions are you experiencing because of the bullying?

2) In what ways are your emotions impacting your work?

3) Do you need help responding calmly and confidently to the bully? Ask a friend to help you practice a disarming response. Select an option from the chapter or one that you have created yourself. Practice saying the phrase in the way you would use it in the workplace. Ask your friend for feedback on how the response sounds and how it might be perceived.

4) What other techniques did you learn from this step that you will start to employ?

Step Four – Maintaining Mental Health

Getting the Support You Need

Step Three took us into the emotional disarray we experience as we're forced to interact with our workplace aggressor every day. During Step Four, you'll learn the importance of supporting your mental health both during the experience and in the months afterward. Many bullying targets do not get the mental health support they need. I don't want that to be the case for you.

One of the reasons you may not seek mental health support immediately is because in the moment, you're trying to keep your job. Your main concern is salvaging your career or reputation from the daily assaults. Your energy becomes consumed with this endeavor while your mental health suffers.

Bullies are experts at separating targets from their workplace support system. You might feel isolated at work because the bully has done a good job of convincing others to turn away from you. Those who normally would have supported you may turn away out of fear of being the next target, or because you appear to be struggling at work. The bully may have mobilized some, or all, of your colleagues into the bullying activity itself. Being targeted by a group is a specific type of bullying designated as *mobbing*. Additionally, consider whether you have isolated yourself due to shame or embarrassment. No matter the reason, suffering from bullying can be a lonely experience.

Despite recent efforts to destigmatize mental health services, some targets still don't seek help because of the stigma. You might believe you are mentally strong. You might believe that this "conflict" at work doesn't rise to the level of needing professional help. But the trauma of workplace bullying is very real. Even after removing yourself from the situation, the fear, anxiety, and even grief from your experience will most likely impact you for years to come. The best thing you can do for yourself is to intentionally seek both informal and formal support networks.

Story - The Emotional Aftermath

After my experience with my grad school supervisor, I returned home. My career plans had been disrupted, so I moved back in with my parents. I took a job as an early childhood teacher and tried to continue with my life. I didn't reapply for school the next semester. *Now what? What should I do?*

Emotionally, I was a mess. My normal cheerfulness and patience became irritation, anger, and impatience. Years later, my mother would recount my demeanor from her perspective. She said, "I didn't know where my daughter had gone, but you were not her."

I had nightmares. Terrible nightmares. I would dream that my grad school supervisor was outside my house in a van waiting to kidnap me. Once I dreamed that they had broken into my house and murdered my parents. I awoke from this vivid dream, called out to my parents, and started to cry when they didn't respond to me immediately. I was sure the dream was true. On one occasion, my mother found me in the living room in the middle of the night with a pair of knitting needles. When she inquired why I was carrying the needles, I told her they were the only "weapon" I had in my room.

My grad school supervisor never overtly threatened me physically. They would often yell, finger point, or trap me in a room, but I didn't label those threats as dangerous or violent. I now know that trapping someone in a room can be considered a type of physical threat. By virtue of their position, my supervisor had achieved control over me and my future.

I was jumpy and almost paranoid at times. I didn't like

staying home by myself. I would hear things outside and become anxious or afraid.

I could sense the difference in my demeanor, and I didn't like the feeling. I realized that I was angry, cynical, anxious, impatient, sad, and on edge. One day at work, I struggled to maintain my patience with the children at the preschool. My supervisor said I needed to talk to someone. She made an appointment for me and drove me there. She'd known me for a year prior to leaving for grad school, and she too had discerned that something wasn't right about the way I was behaving. By the time we got to the appointment, I was hysterically crying. Here I was screwing up again. I was disappointing another supervisor. *Was I going to lose this job too?*

I talked to the therapist. I explained that I'd had a rough year. I told him I had been in grad school and had to return home. I relayed to him that I was trying to decide what to do next. I felt like I had let people down. I felt like I had disappointed everyone around me—my parents, my undergrad professors, and myself. I thought I couldn't "cut it" in grad school.

Interestingly, I never told him about my experience with my grad school supervisor. Why? I wasn't connecting the dots between my experience with my supervisor and what I was feeling now. I was mostly focused on my "failure." I blamed myself for being back home with my life fragmented all around me.

As time went on, I slipped into a depression. My mom tried so many different things to help me. She took me to an acupuncturist. I took herbal supplements that were supposed to help boost feelings of well-being. Eventually, my doctor diagnosed me with mild anxiety and prescribed medication. It helped for the first month or two. I felt better than I had in months, but then I came crashing down and my doctor increased the dosage. The medication made me feel blah—without emotion. I had a hard time making decisions. I didn't have any energy. I suddenly did weird, impulsive things like make Walmart trips at 10:30 at night to buy things that went to live (still in their bags) in the back of my closet. I felt messed up. I felt broken.

During all of this, I did get a new job. I went to work for my alma mater as an admissions counselor. I started to work with people that I knew from my college days. They knew the real me, and I trusted that they cared for me and supported me. Little by little, my confidence grew, and life started to look a little brighter.

With the benefit of hindsight, I had developed post-traumatic stress disorder (PTSD). What I needed was professional counseling. I needed someone to affirm that I had been systematically targeted. I needed someone to help me understand that I had experienced abuse. I needed confirmation that I didn't do anything to disappoint anyone. Along with professional help, I needed the opportunity to demonstrate to myself that I could be successful. This revelation emerged more than two years after I left my grad program. I lost three years of my life to a bully, one year in their presence and the other two immersed in shame, fear, depression, and self-doubt.

After hearing my story, I hope you will seek professional help. Even if you were able to extricate yourself from your situation, you may still be needlessly suffering fears and anxiety. Don't let the bully stop you from living every year of your best life. Don't lose another minute of your life to your abuser.

Navigate Blame, Shame, Fear, and Grief

Blame, shame, and fear are common reactions in workplace bullying. How can workplace bullies be so effective at decimating their targets? Because targets tend to turn the blame inward. The bully counts on our response to be one of self-blame, embarrassment, and shame. Our reaction keeps us focused on our own actions and emotions and off the actions of our aggressors.

Fear is a normal reaction to this experience. There are many things you may fear. You probably fear your aggressor. You fear what will happen next. You fear that the situation will escalate. You are fearful for your job.

You heard elements of *physical fear* in my grad school aftermath. While my supervisor was not physically violent, my nightmares indicated that I absolutely felt my supervisor could do real harm to me even after I moved home 350 miles away. My sense of safety in the workplace was shattered. I had looked forward to continuing my studies and having a rewarding career. Instead, my view of work and the people in charge had drastically changed.

If your aggressor is showing signs of potential physical violence, you should immediately remove yourself from the situation. Notify HR and security of your concerns. As we discussed during Step One, workplace bullies are more likely to be psychologically intimidating than physically. They might step up to the line, but they rarely cross.

One of the most overwhelming feelings for me after both of my experiences was the great sense of loss I felt: not just the loss of a job but loss of future plans, loss of friends and colleagues, and loss of trust in coworkers. Other targets describe grieving the loss of joy in work, loss of a career they loved, and loss of income.

I also felt a tremendous amount of betrayal. I felt betrayed by colleagues who could have helped but didn't. I felt betrayed by an organization that created conditions where a bully's behavior could go unchallenged. I felt betrayed by colleagues who believed and supported the bully instead of me.

Under the weight of all these emotions, you can become quickly overwhelmed. Emotions may persist for years afterward and follow you into future workplaces. Some studies suggest that targets of bullying experience more adverse impacts to their mental and physical health than targets of sexual harassment.[18] The potential damage to you during and after your experience cannot be denied. It's critical that you seek help to support your mental health. In the next section, you'll find informal steps you can take immediately to protect your mental health and discuss where you can find professional help.

Protect Your Mental Health

The emotional work of a formal therapy process can take time. But that doesn't mean you can't take some immediate strides toward a reprieve from the stress caused by the bully. Let's talk about creating space for yourself, setting your boundaries, and being unapologetically selfish.

---

18   M. Sandy Hershcovis and Julian Barling, "Comparing Victim Attributions and Outcomes for Workplace Aggression and Sexual Harassment," *Journal of Applied Psychology* 95, no. 5 (2010): 874–888.

Create Space

Looking back on my workplace experience, I should have immediately taken some vacation to get some distance from my boss and gather my thoughts. Once you realize you are in a situation with a workplace aggressor, take a few days of vacation or sick time.

If you cannot get physical distance outside of work, consider how you might limit your time in the bully's presence while you're at work. This method might be easier if your aggressor is your coworker and not your supervisor, but consider the following options:

- If you have an office, work with your door closed. Or reserve a small conference space in your building to minimize the chance you might bump into each other.
- Find out if you can work from home some or all the time.
- Think about who could attend meetings with you when the bully will also be included. Avoid attending meetings or working alongside the bully alone if possible. Including an ally in the meeting could reduce the chance of abuse, or they may serve as a witness.
- Carry your planner, notebook, or laptop with you. If the aggressor corners you in the hallway, lunchroom, or wherever. Excuse yourself by saying you have "a meeting to get to." This tactic works for remote meetings as well. You can exit to sign on to another meeting or pick up your cell phone, look at it as if it is ringing and just say, "I have to take this call."

Remember that the time the bully is spending abusing you is company time—*unproductive company time.* You have no obligation to sit by and have your time, and the company's time, wasted. Be professional, but make a quick exit if you can. Sitting in front of your abuser and letting them insult or manipulate you is like rolling out the red carpet. They will take their time strolling down that runway if you indulge them. The more face-to-face time you provide your aggressor, the more time they will take to berate you. Anything you can do to limit interactions limits the abuse you'll have to endure.

To get longer term time away, some anti-bully advocates have suggested that targets use their Family Medical Leave Act (FMLA) benefits or work with their doctor to receive long-term disability. If you work for a small company, neither of these options may be available to you. You should be aware that while FMLA gives some protection for your job, it is unpaid and limited to a number of weeks and reasons for how it can be used. Determining whether you are eligible to be on long-term disability can be a lengthy process, and there are no guarantees.

In my experience, taking long-term leave only provides the bully with more space and ammunition for trashing your reputation and laying out a case for your dismissal. I believe the best strategy is to plan to leave your job. The quicker you get started on this process, the less torture you are likely to endure.

Set Boundaries

Take time to set boundaries for yourself. Consider how much you are willing to tolerate. When will you leave the room, the conversation, or the organization? I didn't have the luxury of leaving either of my situations immediately. With my Deceiver bully, I wasn't even clear about all the people involved. I had to put guidelines in place for how I would interact with others in my workplace and still complete my work successfully.

The moment my boss admitted to me that someone had been feeding them information, my workplace became a landmine of potential suspects. Until then, I truly thought that I had underperformed and disappointed my boss. I frequently apologized and worked triply hard to prove that I was capable in my role. I realized it didn't matter what I did; my boss was being swayed by something other than my performance. Then I stopped apologizing. I was done blaming myself for the predicament. Enough was enough. That was the moment I made my decision to exit the organization.

It would take a couple more months before I uncovered who was misrepresenting me. In the meantime, I had to set strict boundaries with all my coworkers. I did not know which one was at fault. I only talked about work. I stopped sharing anything personal. I kept conversations professional but brief.

Setting boundaries around my working hours helped. I'd typically worked a fifty-to-sixty-hour workweek at that job. I eventually established rules for myself regarding work hours. I left at a decent time each day, and I severely restricted the hours I worked on the weekend. I needed time to take care of myself and to apply for new jobs.

Be Unapologetically Selfish

When you are emotionally taxed and exhausted from outmaneuvering the depravity in your workplace, you need to take care of yourself. Don't be afraid to schedule vacation. Don't apologize for taking time for yourself to relax on the weekends.

You need to spend time applying for new jobs, and that task too can be both time consuming and confidence building. Once you have your first application out there, you'll feel more empowered. I remember feeling like I had a secret that was all my own when I enacted my plan to escape.

You are taking hold of what you can control for the good of your health and career. Continue to move forward and call upon your strength. An organization that would allow this abuse to occur doesn't deserve your time or talent. You owe nothing to a person who is morally bankrupt enough to treat you this way.

Seek Professional Help

Creating space, setting boundaries, and being unapologetically selfish may help you in the moment, but you also need to engage professional support. Accessing mental health professionals today has never been easier.

Many employers have Employee Resource Programs (ERPs) or Employee Assistance Programs (EAPs). These programs usually offer free and confidential counseling to employees. They are bound by strict confidentiality and will not reveal usage or services sought to anyone in your organization, including HR. Check your company intranet or make an inquiry to HR to see if your company offers the service. Many of these programs offer more than just counseling, including legal and financial services. So even if you need to call HR to get the information, no one will know why you are requesting the information.

Ask your physician for a referral to counseling services in your area. While you are checking in with your physician, you may want to take note of any other physical symptoms that have emerged recently. Oftentimes stress caused by bullying can manifest into physical health issues. Many targets report issues with sleeping, stomachaches, and headaches.

During my Deceiver encounter, I developed such severe radiating chest pains that my doctor ordered an electrocardiogram. When it came back normal, my doctor asked me if the pain happened at a certain time of the day. I told her most of the time they were during the day while I was at work. She asked me to pay attention to what my body was doing the next time the pain occurred. I discovered that I was hunching my shoulders up toward my ears. When I consciously relaxed my shoulders, the shooting pain subsided. I had become so stressed and tense at work that at times I thought I was having a heart attack. Don't be afraid to talk to your doctor about the stress you are under and how you feel it's impacting your physical health.

Fortunately, we live in a time where there is an app for everything. If you don't feel comfortable going through your company's EAP or asking your doctor for a referral, we all have access to counseling services at our fingertips. Apps like Better-Help and Talkspace allow us to get confidential mental health assistance 24/7 right on our phones.

You can also find a list of additional mental health resources at the back of this book.

Assemble your Support Network

Beyond professional help, your informal support network is just as important. More than likely, your informal help will be located outside of your workplace. Family and friends can be a great source of encouragement. However, beware that some friends may be hesitant to believe you. Those who have not been targets or a witness to workplace bullying can be reluctant to believe it happens. Despite increased awareness over the past twenty-five years, there are still people who either believe it doesn't happen or label it simply "mistreatment."

If someone doesn't recognize your position or thinks you

should just "get over it," move on to another friend who will believe you. Seek out those who will provide the emotional support you need. Choose people that will be able to handle the strong emotions you're experiencing. Engage those who know you well and understand your character and work ethic. Look for allies who will be good listeners, be patient with you, and give you an objective opinion with your best interest in mind. These experiences are emotionally exhausting as well as traumatic. You need someone who will be your sounding board and will not judge you. They will not only let you process emotion but also will know how to nudge you toward taking action if you are hesitant.

Use your support network to . . .

- get clarity around what is happening.
- provide validation that you are a competent professional.
- reassure yourself that you are not paranoid.
- support yourself mentally and emotionally.

Be clear about what you need from your support network. Do you just need someone to listen? Do you need someone to help you make a decision about the situation? Do you need someone to help take your mind off the stress for a little while? When you understand your needs and communicate them, your support network can respond more effectively.

Reflection Questions

These questions were designed to help you make a plan to create some space and build out your support network.

1) How will you get space and time away from the bully? Schedule some vacation now.
2) What boundaries will you set for yourself?
3) Who do you need and/or want in your support network?
4) What you need from your informal support network?
    - Do you need a sympathetic ear?
    - Do you need help looking for new positions?

- Do you need someone who can pull you out of the depths of your emotion and do an enjoyable activity with you each week?

5) Where will you seek professional help? Who will you contact and when?

Step Five –
Protecting Your Career

Escaping the Bully with Your Career Intact

Step Four concentrated on tactics for maintaining your mental health. Step Five focuses on protecting your career and reputation as you plan an exit from your role or from the organization entirely.

I imagine you, like me, take great pride in the reputation you have built throughout your career. You never imagined that anyone would have the power to put your job in jeopardy. In the hands of a bully, your reputation and career path can veer off course quickly. It can be difficult to prevent all damage, particularly if you haven't fully developed your Bully Intelligence.

You need to act quickly to gather documentation and proof of your performance. The documentation will serve several purposes for you as you move into new roles. Amid the discord, many targets don't stop to gather or document information they may need to use for job applications or to protect themselves in an investigation. Taking time to think about what you need during your exit (and beyond) puts you in a place of strength when seeking new employment.

Even if you have not decided to exit just yet or you are trying to work through internal channels to get the behavior to stop, *take these steps anyway.* If there is one thing that you can count on with a workplace bully, it's that they are unpredictable. You never know when someone else will make the decision for you to exit.

I've divided this step into two parts. Part A discusses actions you should take as you are preparing to exit. This involves checking contracts or policies that may need to be addressed before leaving, documenting your experiences properly, and responding to an unfair performance review. And to illustrate how unpredictable a bully's reaction to your exit can be, I'll share a story about my unusual departure from the Deceiver bully.

Part B prepares you to handle interview questions and reference checks as you get ready to move into your next position. There are tips for preparing and handling an exit interview should you choose to provide feedback on your experience to the organization. Then Part B concludes by helping you gain an understanding of how your feelings and attitudes will be altered by your bully experience and what to watch for as you enter a new workplace.

Part A – Prepare for Your Exit

Story - An Unexpected Exit

In the midst of my Deceiver experience, I was exercising my boundaries and diligently working through my exit plan while my boss continually held the threat of demotion over my head. I also discovered that the person I suspected *was* the actual culprit behind my precarious situation.

Eight months after my fateful performance review, I had interviewed for a position, and the new company was starting to check references and run a background check. I knew it was probably just a matter of weeks before I could give my notice. Yet just at that moment, my boss decided that they couldn't supervise me anymore. Instead, they promoted someone else to be my new boss. Yes, it was the snake in the grass that was out to get me all along. My *bully*, the Deceiver, became my *boss*.

I took a deep breath and kept working my plan. Just a few weeks later, I was offered a new position and accepted it. I set up a meeting with both my new and my old supervisors to officially give my notice. My old supervisor looked stunned that I was leaving. My new supervisor (the Deceiver) was so excited, they clapped their hands, high-fived me, and said, "Congratulations!"

Weird . . . right?

My old boss made a quick exit, leaving me alone to work out the details with my latest boss. The ensuing conversation went something like this:

New Boss/The Deceiver:
Well, I bet you are excited to get out of here and start your new position. I think we can get you out of here quickly.

Me: I don't mind staying the two weeks. I want to make sure the transition goes smoothly for all my clients.

New Boss: How long would it take you to talk to the partners and staff?

Me: At least a few days.

New Boss: Open your calendar. According to my research on my new-to-me employees, you have seven days of vacation. If you left on Friday, you could use all your vacation time and be rested to start your new job. [NOTE: This conversation occurred late Wednesday afternoon (and I actually had eleven days of vacation).]

Me: Friday?! (I laughed.) I don't think I can get everything wrapped up in two days, and I have an important client I want to meet with when she is in town next Tuesday.

New Boss: Oh, I am sure we can handle that client for you.

Me: I'm sure you can, but I would like to say goodbye to her in person.

New Boss: I think it would be best if you make a clean break, and we handle it. I don't think you need to stay past Friday.

Me: I still have a few projects that are almost wrapped up. It doesn't make sense to transition them when I can just quickly finish them up.

New Boss: Give me an example of a project that you absolutely must finish yourself that you can't turn over. I think if you go to your office right now, get on the phone, and *apply yourself,* you can be finished and out of here by Friday.

I could see what was going on here. I was being unceremoniously pushed out of the organization. The next morning, I learned my new boss (the Deceiver) had informed my old boss and most of the staff that *I had decided* to be done on Friday. They also reached out to several of my clients and informed them about my departure before I had a chance to do so. I communicated with over forty partners, more than a dozen staff members, wrapped up what little I could, and packed my office in less than two workdays.

For years afterward, I kept my personal files in a box under my desk. I kept my personal items for my desk to a minimum. I couldn't help but remember the unsettling feeling of knowing that I was leaving by my own choice, but that I was thrown out so quickly. I also realize that for someone who is laid off or fired, two days would be a luxurious amount of time.

Why would my new boss do this? Did they think I was on to them?

Maybe. I would learn later that they were setting the stage for unfolding additional drama in the wake of my departure. I could almost hear it, "Well, Dawn left everything in such disarray . . . "

Make the Decision

Let's talk briefly about the decision to leave. Some targets choose to put their head down and soldier on in their position despite the risks. There are legitimate reasons why you might try to stay. Maybe you (or the bully) are close to retirement. Perhaps you know the bully will be transferred soon.

Conceivably, you might be locked into an employment contract and you need to stay to run out the contract. However, the longer you stay in the sights of your aggressor, the more damage to your health and risk to your career.

If you are a union member, you can check your contract to see if there are any provisions that will protect you. In recent years, some union contracts have added anti-bullying language. You may be able to contact your union steward for help in navigating this situation.

I rarely recommend someone try to stick it out, but if you do make that decision, don't wait until the behavior is unbearable before you decide and start working your way out.

Weigh the Option to Confront

Before deciding to leave, you may choose to confront your bully. According to the WBI, 70% of targets attempt to work things out, or even confront, the bully. Yet 93% of those attempts don't stop the behavior.[19] With failure rates this high, I don't recommend confronting as a viable solution for most targets. In the case of my grad school supervisor, I did confront them, and it led to my premature exit from my position. I do believe had I stayed that their behavior would have ramped up.

Prepare for Your Exit

As you start to take steps toward your exit, you'll have mixed emotions. For one, you may feel empowered that you're taking steps to remove yourself from an abusive situation. You can see the light at the end of the tunnel. But at the same time, you may feel sad or angry that you are being forced to leave a job that you love or find rewarding.

When the recruiter called to offer me a new position, away from the grip of the Deceiver, I hung up the phone and I cried. I cried because I was relieved but more so because I realized that I was really going to leave a position that I truly loved.

There are both tactical and emotional steps to take to

---

19   Gary Namie, The Timing and Results of Targets Confronting Bullies at Work (Report No. 2013-D), (Workplace Bullying Institute, 2013), https://workplacebullying.org/download/the-timing-results-of-targets-confronting-bullies-at-work/?wpdmdl=2663&refresh=614771f5434751632072181

prepare for your exit. Career wise, you have been on the job hunt before. Utilize approaches you have had success with in the past. Update your resume and LinkedIn profile, dust off your list of references, and subscribe to job search sites. Engage those in your professional network who may be able to help with your search. Make it clear that your job search needs to be confidential. It's probably best to not share the reason why you are making the leap either. You can just tell them you are ready for something new, and you would appreciate their willingness to keep an eye out for any positions that might be of interest to you.

You might also want to check with your college's career or alumni office. Oftentimes, colleges offer career services for graduates. They may be able to provide you access to job search tools, resume reviews, or even help with interview prep.

Looking for a job can feel like (and turn into) a full-time job. Plan to devote several hours or evenings each week to searching and applying for jobs. Depending on the job market, it may take a while for something to break. But you are a talented professional and, when your search becomes consistent, something will happen for you.

Remember you don't have to settle for only the jobs that are in your geographic area. Consider signing up for a remote job search site like FlexJobs.com

Even if remote work isn't something you want to do long term, remember that you are working to save yourself, your career, and your financial future. Consider whether you can work a remote job for a short period if it gets you away from the bully.

Many people ask me if they should just leave and take any job to get away. While this is always an option, I encourage you to try to find another position aligned with your skills or career plan. If the situation is escalating quickly and you feel you need to take something to get out, then I would advise you to do so.

Targets of bullying often don't feel like they are negotiating from a position of strength in their next job. While the hiring manager or recruiter may not perceive it, you are probably desperate to take the first offer that comes your way. I see targets take positions that pay less than their current salary but are in line with their experience. Taking the cut in pay is tough, but remember, no one is forcing you to stay in that job for twenty years. Think of a move like that as a temporary bridge. It'll buy you some time until you can find your next solid position.

In my case, I was fortunate to be able to take a position that paid about the same and was in line with my professional goals. To some, it may have looked like a step backward. I went from a leadership position to an individual contributor, but as an individual contributor, I had the time to step back from the pressures of leadership and rebound from the previous situation. In retrospect, taking that individual contributor position launched my interest in leadership development and put me in a position to do the work that I do now. And that's work that I truly feel blessed to do. You never know when something that looks like a raw deal on the surface will launch you in a better direction.

Collect Proof of Excellence

Whenever you leave a position (bully or not), you should gather evidence of your excellence as an employee. Things like performance reviews, or projects, processes, policies, and articles that you worked on are tangible proof of your history of good work. As you review these items, you should feel positive about your accomplishments. You have contributed good work for the benefit of your clients and customers. Be proud!

First, gather copies of your performance reviews. If your company conducts annual performance reviews, you should obtain copies of your documents. You should have received a copy of your review, but if for some reason you didn't retain the copy, you can typically get a copy from HR. If your performance review is done in a system, you can often go back into the system and print off a copy yourself. Your reviews can be an excellent way to remind yourself of significant projects, goals, and accomplishments.

Make a list of all the projects you worked on, courses you developed, policies you wrote, and teams you led. Refer to your list when you are polishing your resume and writing cover letters. Are there any artifacts that you can retrieve from those projects? Are you able to print off a copy or take a photo with your phone? Marketing materials for projects are an excellent artifact to get a hold of. I often like to keep outlines of courses I developed or copies of the actual training materials I put together. While you want to be careful of proprietary company information, having examples of your work can be helpful in your job search.

Do you have any emails or notes from your supervisor, colleagues, or clients that sing your praises? Make a copy of these emails or forward them to your personal email. After my negative review, I pulled multiple prior emails from my boss that contradicted what had been said in my review. I requested that the emails be attached to my negative review in my employee file. More on this later.

Check Contracts and Policies

After I made the decision to leave grad school, I received a bill for more than three thousand dollars. This balance popped back onto my account because the registrar said I had not successfully completed my research assistantship. Therefore, I was not entitled to the out-of-state tuition discount that had been originally credited to my account. I argued that the charge should be cleared. According to my assistantship handbook, I had completed the required number of weeks. I checked this clause carefully before I made my decision. I had even consulted the student legal office.

Check any employment contracts that you are covered under. Do you have any other obligations that you might need to deal with as you leave? Paying back tuition assistance is a common obligation that comes to mind. Check on these terms to ensure you aren't surprised by a bill after you leave.

Obtain a copy of the employee handbook. Examine the manual to see if there is a policy or language that prohibits what is happening to you. If there is a policy, it is most likely vague and potentially uses words like *civil* or *respectful* workplace.

Unfortunately, what's happening to you is not illegal, but having a copy of the handbook or policy is helpful in case you do need to seek legal advice. When I received the tuition bill from grad school, I did have a brief consultation with a lawyer. I showed her the language in the student handbook. She told me that although a handbook is not a legally binding contract, it does lay out the expectations for the student-college relationship. She said if we needed to go to court with the student handbook, the college would be crazy to try to fight it. The handbook clearly stated the number of required weeks of assistantship, and I could demonstrate that I had exceeded the number of weeks needed for successful completion. The university eventually relented and removed the charge from my bill.

Gather Documentation

The best thing you can do to protect yourself is to document. If you haven't started to document already, start immediately. If you can remember specific past instances, do your best to document those too. Most situations do not lead to legal action, but if you do want to pursue legal action, documenting is a critical step. You can also use your documentation for an exit interview and leave a record of the behaviors with HR. If they start to see a pattern of behavior, they are more likely to act. Your documentation could be the final ingredient if suspicions are already brewing.

Document the date and time of all incidents. Write down what your aggressor said and any response you made. Document any details that will help with the context of the conversation later on. You may be documenting many incidents over several months, and it can become challenging for you to remember the details of all of the incidents. If there were any witnesses to the conversation, write down those names as well. Witnesses can be supportive allies but don't rely on their willingness to volunteer what they saw or heard. It takes a brave soul to step up. Unfortunately, you can't count on people to place themselves in the line of fire.

Keep your documentation at home. Don't risk your aggressor or someone else seeing your documentation at work (or accuse you of using company time to document).

If the bully has written inappropriate, degrading, or untrue statements in email, make sure that email is part of your documentation. You can forward the email to your personal account, take a screenshot, or take a photo with your phone. Be sure you capture the date and time of the email in your photo. If you do send the emails to your personal account, be sure to print them off regularly and save them in a file or save your documentation to another electronic location. Not long after I left my job, I lost access to my personal email and, with it, several pieces of documentation that I felt were critical to demonstrating what the Deceiver had been doing behind the scenes.

When we are targeted, it is a visceral experience, and we often want to document what these bullying incidents are doing to us emotionally. It's perfectly okay to note how these incidents made you feel. But remember that we can't solely focus on the impact to us personally. We need to also document the impact *to the business*. If we can consistently show employers how the *organization* is being harmed by this person's behavior, we increase the chances that action will be taken.

Being able to think about the impact to the business may take some mental gymnastics, especially when you are feeling so emotionally raw. Here are a few things to think about in terms of impact.

Did the bully's behavior . . .

- delay work?
- distract others?
- waste time?
- reduce the quality of the work?
- result in a lost customer or contract?
- result in employee turnover?

When I left grad school, I wanted to express my anger at the way I was treated. I went right to the top and wrote a letter to the university president. Below is a snippet from my letter:

> *From day one, the other assistants and I suffered degradation at the hands of our supervisor. By their treatment we came to believe we were incompetent and unmotivated.*

My statement above is true and accurately portrays how I felt. I now have a greater understanding that the president wouldn't act on one grad student's emotions. Consider how differently this rewritten paragraph might have been received by the university president.

From day one, our supervisor withheld training and support necessary to do our jobs. This resulted in additional hours being billed to the project to correct errors in the data. The overall accuracy of the data is questioned by most, if not all, involved in the research. Inaccurate research data may impact the interventions derived from the data and ultimately could damage the university's reputation for data and research integrity.

Yes, I know this second version is *completely unsatisfying* as a target, but I suspect the university president might have been more interested in acting on behalf of the integrity of his university.

The business impact matters. If we're going to change organizational thoughts on the impact of bullying, we need to speak in terms of how the business is damaged if the bully is allowed to continue their behavior.

Respond to an Unfair Review

If you recall from my story about my unfavorable review, my boss asked me if I agreed with my review and told me to sign off on the document. I didn't know at the time, but when you sign your review (either with an actual signature or an electronic signature), most of the time you are *only* acknowledging that the review has been shared with you. By signing, you are *not* acknowledging any agreement with the content of the review.

You also have the right to respond to a review that you think is unfair. You can request that your response be attached to the review and kept in your employee file (paper or electronic). I prepared a multi-page response to my review. It included a letter, a list of my accomplishments for the year in question, and copies of several emails from my supervisor. The emails expressed the opposite of what they'd stated in my review.

Here is an example of a review rebuttal letter:

From: Your name and title
To: Your Supervisor
Cc: Human Resources (if applicable) or your supervisor's

leader (if you so choose)
Re: Performance Evaluation for the year XXXX
Date: Date of letter

Please consider this my formal response to my performance evaluation held on (date of review meeting). I am exercising my right as an employee to have this letter of rebuttal attached to my performance evaluation and placed within my employee file until such time as the negative evaluation is removed from my file.

I believe in the mission of (organization name). I enjoy my work, my coworkers, and our clients. I am a good employee. I consistently put in the extra time and effort it takes to work in our organization. The accomplishments I achieved throughout my years of service reflect my commitment, enthusiasm, and capability. (You might choose to list a few accomplishments here.)

As an employee, I expect and welcome timely feedback on my performance. The results of this review took me aback. It is my purpose with this letter to list the facts in terms of my actual achievements within the last performance cycle.

I am appreciative that you recognized in my review my commitment to the organization, my attention to detail, my ability to follow through, and the specialized knowledge that I contribute to the organization. (Use this paragraph to highlight if there were any bright spots listed in the review itself.)

I have worked hard, and I will continue to do so. I welcome discussion and any specific suggestions for improvements that you can recommend to enhance my performance in the future.

Attached to this letter are a list of accomplishments, challenges, and additional key roles I have assumed. In addition, I have attached several email communications. In the emails, you express that my performance is meeting and even exceeding your expectations, which is not in line with what you expressed to me in my review.

Thank you.

Respectfully submitted,
Your Name and Signature

Each person's situation is different. In my case, I found it empowering to write this letter because I felt that my truth had been ignored. You'll ultimately need to decide for yourself if responding to your review is of benefit to you.

Part B –
Prepare for Your Next
Position

Preparing for another position, especially if you have been in your current position or at your current workplace for a long time, can be intimidating. Not only do you have to deal with the nerves around interviews, portfolios, and presentations as parts of the normal search process, but you always have the reason for your search in the back of your mind. Targets can start to feel a little desperate, which can make every interview feel life-and-death critical.

This part starts with how to confidently answer interview questions that can be hurdles for bully targets. Then it dives into tips to make a smoother transition into a new role, some of which you might not have expected.

Practice Interview Questions

Interviewers will ask you questions about your current work performance and relationships, which can be triggering for someone who is currently in or has just come out of a traumatic work situation (like bullying). You can easily be tripped up by seemingly innocuous interview questions.

In one interview I was in, I was asked to describe a conflict I had with a previous supervisor and how I had worked to re-solve that conflict. My brain immediately went to the situation with my negative performance evaluation and all the drama that ensued. I panicked. I searched my brain for another exam-ple of a conflict. I went so far back in my work history to pull a safe example that the job was no longer listed on my resume. When the interviewer tried to place the conflict in relation to my resume, I had to explain that the scenario was in the distant past. They then asked, "Well, is there anything else that isn't on your resume that you would like to tell us about?" They clearly didn't believe me and probably would not be sympathetic to my experience. The question had caught me off guard, and I was embarrassed that I was unable to answer it well.

You want to answer interview questions honestly *and* pro-fessionally. You don't want your emotions to catch you off guard in an interview. You also don't want to indicate the level of con-flict you experienced in your previous workplace. It's not advis-able to bad-mouth your previous employer. These are all reasons to be prepared. Practice your answers out loud to questions like the examples below. I have provided you with some ideas for safe and honest answers to each of these questions:

- Why are you leaving your current position?
- Tell me about the traits of your ideal supervisor.
- If I were to ask your previous supervisor (or colleague) about your best work habits/skills, what would they say?
- Tell me about a time you had a conflict at work. What was the conflict about, and how did you resolve the conflict?
- Tell me about a time when you received negative feedback. How did you handle receiving the feedback, and how did you make improvements to your performance?

Why are you leaving your current position?

This question can be answered by simply stating "it's time for a change." No one expects people to stay with a company for thirty years anymore. It's not unusual for someone to want to change jobs or even industries. Stating "I am seeking a new challenge" or "this position intrigues me" are also safe, honest, and acceptable answers. Avoid mentioning conflict, abuse, challenges with your colleagues, supervisors, or the work.

I have sat on interview committees when the candidate has answered this question with "I need to get away from my boss" or "I'm not being treated well at my current employer." I always cringe a bit when I hear those answers. The answers may be the truth, but those candidates rarely make it through to the next round. Why? The interviewers make a natural assumption that this employee may be difficult to work with or may struggle with representing themselves professionally. I believe that some employers ask this question not because it is important for them to know, but because they are gauging your professionalism with respect to your employer.

Tell me about the traits of your ideal supervisor.

This question may seem simple and straightforward, but if the aggressor you are trying to get away from is your supervisor, the first traits that pop into your head are the ones that you *don't want* in a supervisor. Think about this one beforehand so you have a few traits top of mind. Do you value honesty? Fairness? Do you want a supervisor who cares about your growth and development? Do you prefer a supervisor who can give straightforward feedback? There isn't a wrong answer to this question. You just want to be prepared to explain those positive preferences when you are asked. The employer is often looking for alignment between your desired traits and the temperament of the hiring manager.

If I were to ask your current supervisor (or colleague) about your best work habits/skills, what would they say?

By asking this question, your potential employer is gauging your self-awareness along with positive traits you bring to the table. Be prepared and don't use any of the perceptions outlined by your aggressor. Consider offering skills specific to your industry or just general effective workplace skills like "attention to detail," "follow-through," or "ability to balance multiple priorities."

Tell me about a time you had a conflict at work. What was the conflict about and how did you resolve the conflict?

Everyone has conflict. This is a normal natural outcome of asking human beings with differing ideas and skill sets to work together. Do not be tempted to avoid the subject all together and say, "I haven't had conflict with someone at work." No one will believe you. Select real examples you have experienced of common types of workplace conflict. Here are a couple of examples to jump-start your brainstorming:

- You and a colleague had differing ideas on how something should be done.
- There was a misunderstanding on the team about who was responsible for completing a task.
- A decision was made that some people didn't agree with.

Tell me about a time when you received constructive feedback. How did you handle receiving the feedback, and how did you make improvements to your performance?

Next to the question about why you are leaving your current employer, I think this is the toughest question for those who have had a workplace bullying experience. Because the bullying comments and context center around our work's quality, we essentially interpret it as negative feedback. Because the experience is so emotional, our brains will take us naturally to the "feedback" from the bully.

Employers ask this question to get a sense of your ability to graciously accept feedback and put it into action. For this question, prepare a couple of examples of innocuous pieces of feedback you have received in the past and how you worked to respond. Here are a few examples to consider:

- Feedback on production (e.g., increasing your skill level to deliver higher quality, increasing speed without reducing quality)
- Feedback on working with clients/customers (e.g., giving an effective sales pitch, handling customer service issues)
- Feedback on giving a presentation (e.g., reducing "ums and ahs," answering questions with brevity)
- Feedback on running a meeting (e.g., preparing a proper agenda, managing time, allowing others time to speak)

While it is preferable that they are recent examples, they don't have to be from your current workplace.

Remember that the hiring team is on your side. They are not intentionally trying to trip you up. They are asking questions to help you explain your experiences and accomplishments. The person who interviews the best isn't the one who answers the quickest or who has the longest or most detailed responses. The purpose of the interview is to ask questions so a candidate can thoughtfully put into words how their experience could benefit the employer. Pause and think if you need to, and take a sip of water if you need an extra moment to gather your thoughts. Being a successful candidate is about preparing with intention.

Understand Reference Checks and Job Verification

When targets of bullies get to the point of being a finalist for a new position, they discover one additional hurdle that makes them extremely nervous. That hurdle is the reference check. People trying to get out of a bad situation ask me if their current work or current bully (if the bully is their boss) can completely derail their chances for a new position in the final stages of a job search. Let me ease some anxiety immediately and say that the short answer is no.

Some people become nervous because on some job applications, the potential employer asks you to list all your past supervisors and their contact information. In recent years, I've noticed that many online applications are not asking for any supervisor contact information. Why? Probably because they never used that information.

A potential employer should never contact your current employer without your permission. I did have one potential employer that wanted to call my then-current supervisor. When they asked for my permission, I asked if I was the final candidate. The recruiter said I was one of two candidates. I explained that I did not want to upset my supervisor by letting them know that I was looking if they weren't offering me the job. The recruiter said that they understood completely and honored my request. I was later offered the job. My request didn't impact my chances for the position. It's unusual that a potential employer would want to talk to your current supervisor as a part of the job selection process. Most people don't want to tip their hand to their current employer while they're looking.

A potential employer may check your personal references. Your personal references are the people that you select and give the employer permission to contact. You don't need to have a current supervisor or colleague on your list of references. You are in control of choosing people who know you well and will give you a positive reference.

The employer may also do an employment verification. The verification is typically done through the HR department and not through your supervisor or anyone in your department. The recruiter will typically ask to verify the dates of employment you have listed on your resume or application. They may also ask if you are eligible for rehire. If you left on your own or were laid off, you're usually considered eligible for rehire. If you were fired, you may be classified as ineligible for rehire. The HR department cannot release any other performance or personnel information other than the dates of employment and rehire eligibility.

Consider an Exit Interview

Most organizations have some type of exit interview process. It may be in the form of a survey they send you after you've left the organization. It may also be an actual interview with someone from HR.

Whether you want to participate in the exit interview process is always voluntary. What you say and how much you reveal in the process is always up to you as well. Data collected in exit interviews is typically only reported to company leaders in aggregate. Comments may also be reported but are not attributed to any one employee. Comments are often useful to try to spot negative trends with a leader or within a specific area of the company. If employees who have negative experiences never tell anyone, the problems go on for years and other employees fall victim.

I understand why some people choose not to participate in an exit interview. You may still be experiencing some fear that your bully or company officials will have power over your future career. Despite interview data and employee performance being confidential, there can still be a fear that word will get out in a small community.

If your company doesn't have an exit interview process, you can still request one with HR. After the situation with my performance review, I requested an exit interview. In addition to the HR person, I asked that my original boss be present. Since there were no formal interview questions, I spent some time thinking about what I wanted to say. I brought my notes because I didn't want to forget any of my points. I asked them both to just listen while I got my thoughts out and they could ask questions or make comments at the end. They honored my request.

While I don't think my exit interview made much of a difference, I'm glad that I had a chance to tell my side of the story. The exit interview is your opportunity to share your viewpoint with no fear of retribution. If you've documented a strong pattern of behavior that has been ignored, this is your chance to provide all that documentation to HR. Even if the documentation didn't save you, it may save someone else from a similar fate.

Don't let the bully keep you distracted. Keep your focus on doing what you need to do to protect yourself. I found strength and hope from being able to maintain some control over what was happening with my career when everything else at work was so out of control.

Anticipate a Bumpy Reentry

By now, hopefully you've made some decisions and made a plan to move away from your aggressor. Congratulations on taking the first steps to breaking free both physically and mentally from the bully!

Before we leave this section on career, I want to prepare you for the fact that your experience of being bullied will change the way you experience work. The way you view co-workers and your supervisors will be different. The amount you share at work may change. You may not be able to tolerate as much stress as you did in the past. You might feel burned out and prefer to work in a less demanding job. Going to work may continue to bring you some fears and anxiety (at least for a little while).

Remember that you aren't the same person you were in your previous position. You can't continue to work in the same way you always have. You will mourn the loss of the old you— the you that was more trusting, more social, and more carefree at work. This is a hard reality for many targets to accept.

After I left the Deceiver, I landed in a good place, both career wise and financially. I still mourned the loss of my previous role for months. I missed the work. I missed the clients. I missed working with many of my coworkers. I had a hard time making connections with my new colleagues. I wasn't crazy about the work I was doing. I was a little leery of getting too attached to the people, the place, or the work. I didn't have a high level of trust in my new coworkers (even though they had given me no reason not to trust them). I idealized my previous workplace. *Maybe it wasn't that bad?*

Many targets wrestle with changes in their career aspirations after their experience. It's not uncommon for a leader who was bullied to seek out an individual contributor position for their next immediate role. Taking a position that has less responsibility can be a welcome change (at least temporarily).

I often advise targets to remember that just because they may have landed somewhere does not mean they are destined to stay there forever. This position can be just a layover—a place of respite—while looking for something more aligned with your interests or income needs. Sometimes you need to take that position to get out; keep in mind that being away from the bully can create several positive effects: a clearer head, improved health, and more energy and mental capacity.

Targets may find themselves with a negative perception of an entire organization or industry based on their experience. I have known targets who never return to their prior industry and some who never do work at the level they were at again. This fact greatly impacts their enjoyment of their career and their earning potential.

Targets often develop triggers. A *trigger* is a behavior or perception that brings back emotions or raises red flags for the target. I have two triggers that get activated quite a bit in the workplace. One is gossip. As I mentioned during Step Two, I should have realized that it was likely that the person who was sharing gossip *with me* was also likely sharing gossip *about me*. We all engage in gossip in the workplace at some point. But if I see someone who can't hold a confidence and always seems to want to dish some dirt on someone, I make a mental note to watch my interactions with that person and avoid them if possible.

A second trigger for me is around what I would call "administrative work." My supervisor, during my negative performance review threatened to demote me. They told me I could "stay on and do administrative work." Putting me in this position (or the perception of this position) even now, still triggers emotion. Now please don't misunderstand—I'm capable and perfectly happy doing the supporting functions that underlie my position. I don't think that I'm above making appointments, reserving rooms, ordering meals, making lists, or tracking attendance. In fact, I do these functions every week as a part of my current job (because that's what happens in a small department), but if someone intentionally and repeatedly makes requests of me that make me feel like I'm becoming their admin, it makes me frustrated. That doesn't mean that I get angry, yell, or tell them to do it themselves (although sometimes I would like to). By being aware of my triggers, I can understand why I am feeling a certain emotion. And I'm much less likely to get worked up over it if I know where it is coming from. Consider your potential triggers as you go into a new work environment.

My first performance review in my new job was a nerve-racking experience. Not because my new boss did anything to make me wary but because my previous experience had been so traumatic. I fretted for weeks beforehand. I barely slept the night before the review. During the meeting, though, my new supervisor had nothing but good things to say about how quickly I had gotten up to speed, the high ratings I was getting from my students, and how much trust and respect my new colleagues had for me. I came out of the review both shocked and beaming. I called my mom, and I cried. I told her, "My supervisor says that they could not have asked for more out of a new person and that I was a model employee."

My mom replied, "Because you are a good employee. What happened at your last review was wrong. I hope you can start to believe in yourself again." Over time, I did start to believe in myself again, but I won't lie, performance reviews still make my heart skip a beat.

After both of my experiences, I carried a variety of fears into the next workplace. I feared "getting in trouble" with my boss. I feared that I could be fired (or my job could be threatened). I was afraid that people in my new workplace would find out what happened. I also feared people would hear what was said about me and they would believe the lies. For a time, I was even scared of those in leadership roles. Now more than ever, I understood how much power they had over me, my career, and my financial future.

After my grad school experience, I never imagined that I could have another bad experience like that again, but my

Deceiver situation changed that perception. While the fear of being targeted again is uncomfortable, it certainly serves a purpose. Fear can remind us of the lessons we learned. It can help us be more cautious as we enter new workplaces with new people, especially until we can determine who we can trust. While fear doesn't need to be our constant companion, know that it could be hanging around for a bit after you move on to your next job.

Changing jobs can feel daunting, but taking steps to prepare yourself for the process and getting into the right mindset for the transition should ease the intimidation factor.

All aspects of this step focused on practical tips to prepare for the transition to your next position. In the next step, we'll discuss ways to heal and rebuild confidence.

Reflection Questions

The first three reflection questions for this step are tactical. They help you list the items you need to make your transition. The final two questions prompt you to consider how to document your experience so you can leave it with your organization. Work through questions one through three first. You can return to the final two questions when you are closer to making your exit.

1) What do you need to prepare to start your job search? Is your resume updated? Your LinkedIn profile? Make a list and schedule time in your evening calendar to update and polish anything you'll need to apply to new positions.

2) What artifacts do you need to gather for your proof of excellence? Make a list of all the items and a timeline to gather the artifacts.

3) What will you document going forward? You can use the template in the companion workbook to record all the necessary information.

4) How would you describe the bully's impact on the business?

5) What would you say in an exit interview?

Step Six –
Believing in Yourself

Rebuilding Your Confidence and Resilience

As we move out of Step Five and into Step Six, let's keep the focus on you. This step emphasizes specific strategies for increasing your confidence and rebuilding your resilience.

Following each of my experiences, I would describe myself as an exhausted shell of who I was. I had a hard time understanding how these bullying experiences could happen to me. I couldn't change the past, but I was now fully in control of my future. A part of me would never be the same, though. I had to figure out what good could emerge from a horrible reality. After being in an aggressive workplace situation, you can decide to accept what is and where you landed, and you can choose to rise again. You and only you can take steps to work on building yourself back up.

Many targets don't recognize the changes that the experience makes to their confidence both as a person and as a professional. They may start second guessing themselves or suddenly need constant assurance where they once didn't. The level of insecurity can impact success in future roles if allowed to continue unchecked.

Emotional reserves are often depleted after any bullying encounter, but an especially intense or long encounter can be particularly exhausting. A target may be less able to handle everyday stressors as resilience levels are low and need to be replenished.

The good news is that you don't have to wait to begin regaining your confidence or rebuilding your resilience. Specific practices that you can execute will make you feel stronger. Invest in yourself by taking the time to develop an intentional routine to strengthen your confidence. Be patient with yourself. Recovery from your experience, like any other trauma, will take time.

Believe in Yourself

Even after months away from my aggressors, I recognized their words in my head. Despite all the evidence to the contrary, I believed their words. Words are powerful—they can lift us up, or they can destroy us. The words that my boss said to me during my performance review struck at a core part of my identity that proved hard to recover from.

My boss was someone I trusted and whose opinion I'd respected. I couldn't get their words out of my head: *no leadership skills, couldn't get along with people,* and *struggled to represent the organization.* Those words eroded essential beliefs I had about myself. Even as I studied leadership in my master's program and worked with leaders as a part of my day job, I could hear the words of my supervisor in my head. *Was it true? Was I a fraud?* I lived in fear that someone would find out what they said. Worse yet, I feared someone would believe those words.

The supervisor in my new job nominated me for a community leadership program. I was nervous. *Would someone know I really shouldn't be there?*

But then it dawned on me. No one knew about my past. This program was an opportunity to make a new start. It was a chance to rebuild my confidence and shift the beliefs that my boss had branded in my brain. I had to consciously push my boss's words and actions aside and replace them with positive thoughts and success-filled experiences.

The first day of the leadership program, I challenged myself to volunteer for an activity. I wanted people to see me again. Not the person I had become—tentative, anxious, and insecure. Not the person who didn't believe in herself and thought she had gotten what she deserved. I graduated from the program and went on to serve on the program's advisory board for six years. The whole experience was an opportunity to rediscover me—a creative, compassionate, collaborative employee and *leader.*

Shortly after graduating from the leadership program, I was recruited into a full-time position where I would go on to train and advise several hundred leaders. By then, I knew what good leadership was and had realized that my previous boss didn't know what they were talking about.

I now have a plaque that hangs on the outside of my home office door: BELIEVE IN YOURSELF. I remember the day I found it in a gift shop. I was struck by both its simplicity and its power. Every morning, it's a reminder as I walk into my office, telling me where I've been and who I've become, and to never forget the lessons that I learned. I must believe in myself first and not let others' words overshadow my belief in myself.

Purge Words and Emotions

If you are having a hard time letting go of the words that your aggressor put in your head, try this exercise that I did after I returned from my disastrous grad school experience. It had been almost a year since I left grad school, and I was still struggling. I'm not sure where this idea came from, but I decided to write a letter to my grad school supervisor. I wasn't going to send the letter. I just wanted to use the letter as an exercise to purge my negative feelings. The letter went something like this:

Dear *,*

I am writing you this letter to purge all the bad feelings, fear, and hatred I have for you. I feel very sorry for you. I am sorry you have not achieved your goals and are stuck in a job that is not your ideal. I am sorry for whatever tragedy occurred in your lifetime that caused you to become so bitter and hateful. You know what though, no matter what happened to you in the past or is trapping you in your present, it does not give you the right to treat anyone the way you treated me. It does not give you an excuse to not do your job to the best of your ability. It does not give you the right to place blame on others for your misfortunes or mistakes. It does not give you permission to oppress and destroy the spirit.

How dare you think that I am inferior to you. If anything, you are a peon to my compassionate superiority. I do not care what you think of me. Your opinion isn't worth dirt. I know that I am intelligent, capable, compassionate, and determined. My own opinion is the only one that matters.

Every day in your presence caused me to sink deeper and deeper into an emotional hole. Away from you, the fear, the anger, and the paranoia did not dissipate. A year has passed, and I am writing to tell you that no more will you cause me pain. I will not waste one more of my beautiful days on this earth wallowing in the memory of what you did to me. You destroyed a part of me. You took everything that I believed to be good and fair and true about the workplace, and you shattered it. No more will you throw dirt down on me and laugh as I cower. I will succeed in this world despite you. I will heal the wounds you caused. The memory of every insult that you hurled at me will no longer stand in my way of my relationships, my career, or my own feelings about myself.

You may have ripped apart my trust in others, but you cannot take away my education, and you did not steal my enthusiasm or my ambition for education and success. Strange as it sounds, I also thank you. You opened my eyes to a tragic experience for some college students. I am determined to defend and protect other students from the likes of people like you. I will not let another bully break the spirit of another Dawn.

My wishes for revenge upon you have fatigued me. I will no longer waste my energy being a vengeful person for that would be stooping to your level. I believe in my heart that someday your words and actions will catch up with you, and that is enough to satisfy me.

Dawn

Okay. Maybe it was *exactly* like that. I found a copy on my computer when I was going through files in preparation for writing this book. It might feel a tad over-dramatic—I was only twenty-three at the time.

After I wrote the letter, a family friend invited my family over for a campfire. I read the letter, then ripped and crumpled it before throwing it into the fire. It was a public declaration that I was ready and *needed* to move on from this experience. It was also a symbolic destruction of the bully's words. Was I immediately changed for the better? Did I go back to my normal self the next day? No. But it was one step closer to breaking free from the negativity of the experience, which empowered me to focus more on my future.

Write your letter. It doesn't have to be professional. It doesn't have to be grammatically correct. It just must express what you are feeling. It's all for your benefit. Burn your letter, rip it up, send it through your shredder or whatever destruction feels good to you. Please don't send your letter. Better to symbolically burn your negative emotions than to actually burn bridges.

Recall Your Success

Now that you're starting to let go of the bully's words, let's begin filling your head with memories of success. A relatively simple yet powerful practice is to make a daily (or weekly) habit of recalling your successes. Looking at or reading items that remind you of your success and your accomplishments will help you feel more positive.

Since my very first job out of college, I've kept what I call a "smile file" in my desk. When I get a thank-you note from a client or a positive email from a colleague, I print it out and put it in my smile file. When the days really got bad with my boss and the Deceiver, I'd grab my smile file and read the contents. It reminded me of the good I was doing and my contributions to my clients' lives. It was proof to me that I was a good employee. In addition to creating your own smile file, here are a few simple ways to keep your success top of mind.

- Make an accomplishment list. List all the projects you are proud of, awards and accolades you have received, schooling you have completed, and anything else you can think of that makes you feel accomplished or confident. Keep your list somewhere in your home where you will see it each morning or throughout the day.

- Write a success journal. In your journal, recall previous successes as well as the challenges you had to overcome. Write about the current challenges you are facing and the steps you are taking to create the best possible outcome for yourself.
- Review your positive performance reviews, reference letters, and any other documents you have that sing your praises.
- Ask a friend or colleague to have a conversation with you about your good qualities.
- Surround yourself with words that inspire you (music, quotes, books, etc.).

Recalling your success generates the positive emotions to balance out the negative thoughts the bully plants in your head. It's easy to hear critical words in the moment and believe them despite all the evidence to the contrary. Place more significance on your years of success than on the bully's words. Practicing positive and healthy thinking is a vital part of self-care and building resilience. Let's tackle those concepts next.

Prioritize Self-Care and Rebuild Resilience

During and after both of my experiences, I struggled to maintain my normal healthy routines. I overate and ate junk. I didn't feel like exercising, so I didn't. My sleep was disturbed for a variety of reasons. Taking care of myself just wasn't a priority when my work life was in shambles. When I got home, all I wanted to do was sit on my couch and get absorbed in a mind-numbing television show or a game on my phone. You may feel the same way I did.

Recently, I discovered research about resilience and our ability to influence our own level of resilience. *Resiliency* is our ability to "bounce back" from stress, trauma, and challenging situations.[20] The strength of our resilience allows us to adapt and recover when we are faced with difficult times.

After leaving an aggressive workplace situation, I can almost guarantee that most of your resilience resources will be depleted.

20   David Palmiter et al., "Building Your Resilience," American Psychological Association, 2012.

Whether you are currently in the midst of a situation right now or you are recovering from one, engaging in intentional exercises can help you bounce back from the situation more quickly.

A perfect metaphor for our resilience is a balance scale. Imagine your scale with all your stress and trauma on one side, and on the other side are your support networks and tools you use to maintain your physical and mental health. When the stressors on one side of the scale become greater than our tools and support on the other, our scale tips. Our resilience can wax and wane throughout our lifetime, but we can maintain and even rebuild our resilience with some simple practices.

There are four actions that researchers and mental health professionals have identified as keys to rebuilding your resilience:

- Nurture positive connection
- Focus on finding meaning
- Practice healthy thinking
- Prioritize wellness[21]

I wish I would have had these tools in my hands while I was recovering from my encounters. I believe I would have been able to move forward more quickly. Here's what I recommend for applying them during and after your workplace bully ordeal.

Nurture Positive Connection

In the context of building resilience, there needs to be a balance between the negative, draining interactions and the positive interactions. Earlier, I shared some tactics for getting space from your aggressor if you can. As you reduce the number of negative interactions, building up the number of positive interactions you're experiencing is equally important.

Who are the colleagues, friends, and family that you admire for their resilience and positivity? Make it a priority to spend some time with them each week. You can accomplish this by scheduling time with them to go to coffee, talk on the phone, or go for a walk.

---

21   Adapted from Palmiter et al., "Building Your Resilience."

During Step Four, we talked about the people who could be part of your bullying support network. I encourage you to develop a supplemental support network. Your supplemental support network doesn't have to know anything that is going on with you at work. In fact, connecting with this segment of your support network can be a refreshing break from thinking and talking about your challenges at work. Keep the conversation focused on the positive—future plans, happy memories, and funny stories. Connecting with these folks will give your brain a much-needed break from the craziness that's consuming most of your life. Do your best during these times to let the stress at work fall to the back of your mind. These moments enable you to recharge and maybe even gain some new perspectives on your situation.

Take note of how you feel both before and after these interactions to gauge how effective the practice is for you. Reflect on how spending time with different people makes you feel. Make an intentional plan to engage more with people who help your energy soar. They help you navigate and survive your current situation even if they don't know anything about it.

In both of my encounters, I had both a support network that knew about the bullying and a network that did not know about the bullying. I wasn't disciplined enough to leverage them in the right way. I didn't let my brain "get away" from thinking and talking about work. At times, I believe I was in real danger of alienating some segments of my support network. Rather than spending time ruminating, spend time with your supplemental support network doing things that bring you joy. Plan something every week that you can look forward to with one of your friends—dinner, a hike, a movie night, etc.

Some of my friends instinctively knew that I needed a distraction and would invite me to do things with them. I am grateful they were so wise. But I encourage you to be proactive and schedule these intentional break times. Having something fun to anticipate each week will help you through the turmoil.

Focus on Finding Meaning

The second area of focus to build resilience has to do with your purpose. For many of us, our work is how we leave our mark on the world. Being successful at work is tied not only to our financial success and well-being but also our sense of self-worth. The moment you became a target, your aggressor took away any joy that you found in your work. The bully has now made you doubt the significance of your contributions.

Our work gives us a sense of purpose. It brings meaning to our lives. Suddenly, with our bully's voice in our head, we can't focus on finding the meaning in our work. We find ourselves just focused on maintaining our job and trying not to collapse into a weeping mess on the floor.

Finding meaning in our everyday life is important for resilience because it connects us to purpose. When our work life is in sudden disarray, we need to uncover the smaller moments that tap into that feeling of purpose. You may need to think more broadly about what you find meaningful. Meaning may quickly shift more toward your life outside of work. Consider questions like, "Were you able to help someone today?" or "Did you take a step toward a personal goal?"

Documenting these moments may amplify their benefit to you. Research from the University of Minnesota found that people who wrote down two or three positive things at the end of their workday had lower stress levels and felt calmer in the evening.[22] The act of reflecting on some positive aspects of your day can again help your brain stay out of the anxiety-ridden path it's currently on. Some days will be easier than others. Some days, the only positives might be, "I only had to be in one meeting with the bully today." The more you retrain your brain to recognize even the most minor of positives in your day, the easier it will become. In fact, you might find yourself listing more than three things that are positive despite the situation.

Another practice that might be helpful is getting up in the morning and thinking about what you *do* get to do that day that will be positive and meaningful for you. You might even consider adding these highlights to the top of your calendar or posting them somewhere you can see them throughout the day.

Walking through the disorienting fog of being bullied can

---

22   Joyce E. Bono and Theresa M. Glomb, "The Powerful Effect of Noticing Good Things at Work," *Harvard Business Review*, September 4, 2015.

make it extremely difficult for you to think positively. Being intentional about declaring or reflecting on meaningful events or acts from the day will help you see the sun peek out from behind the clouds.

Practice Healthy Thinking

Expanding on the concept of finding the positive in your day, healthy thinking is another key focus area for building resilience. I am not a counselor or an expert in the way the brain reacts to stress and anxiety, but it's my understanding that when we focus on negative thoughts, our brain creates, for lack of a better word, ruts. Our brain finds it easy to travel along those ruts, which causes us to ruminate on the thoughts that created the ruts in the first place.

If you are focused on your aggressor's words, your brain is creating a nice, deep rut surrounding those negative thoughts. You will struggle to stop your brain from the habit of settling into that rut unless you engage in some intentional practice to shift your thinking.

Bullies would like nothing more than for targets to fully take to heart all the lies they are dishing out. They revel in the ability to disrupt work and personal life. If you let their words settle into your head, even if you extricate yourself physically, the bully will still have a hold on you at some level.

Leveraging healthy thinking to build your resilience means that you want to stay hopeful despite your circumstances. You want to keep what's happening to you in the right perspective. Remind yourself that this won't last forever, especially if you have already taken steps to move yourself out. If you are outside your bullying situation already, healthy thinking might mean reflecting on what lessons you can take away from the experience.

Some mental health experts recommend their clients develop a resilience toolkit.[23] To create a toolkit, make a list of five to ten activities that you enjoy doing. When you feel yourself slipping into a negative space, commit to reviewing your list and doing one of the activities. Doing something pleasurable

23   Mental Health Commission of Canada, "COVID-19 Self-care and Resilience Guide," *Mental Health First Aid Canada* (blog), March 24, 2020.

should help your brain jump out of the rut. Here are some examples of activities you might put on your list:

- Going for a walk or working out
- Spending 20 minutes working on a jigsaw puzzle
- Spending 30 minutes reading a novel
- Listening to your favorite music playlist (you might even be able to do this at work depending on your work culture/rules)
- Talking to a friend
- Taking a bath
- Going outside for some fresh air

To learn more about creating your own resilience toolkit, refer to the resource list in the back of the book.

The first three resilience building focus areas center around your mindset: seeking out connections that generate a sense of optimism, looking for ways to ground yourself in purpose, and focusing your brain on healthy thoughts will build your sense of mental well-being. These actions work together with your efforts to recall your success to boost your confidence and give you the courage to keep moving forward.

Physical health also plays a key role in our strength and stamina. It's hard to maintain mental wellness if we aren't physically well. That brings us to the final resilience focus area—physical wellness.

Prioritize Wellness

Maintaining your physical health is the fourth focus area of resilience. Our mental and physical selves are unavoidably linked. When we aren't feeling well physically, we'll find it more difficult to focus on the positive aspects we need to keep up our resilience. When we aren't mentally feeling well, we don't have the energy to push ourselves to do the things we should do to keep our body well like exercising or cooking a healthy meal.

To stay strong in the face of this challenge, you need to keep your body strong. Take time for yourself each day. Eat a healthy diet and exercise. Get regular sleep. Consider taking up a mindfulness practice or simply pause to do some deep breathing every day. Remember to take days off as you need them to rejuvenate your mind and body.

Recognize Your Strength

In my town, there's an art glass shop where you can stop in and watch the glass artists at work. Throughout the year, you'll see a crowd gathered around the front window of the shop, watching the process of glass going into the big ovens, then being carefully crafted into beautiful artistic shapes. After the intense heat of the oven and the stress and pressure of being blown and shaped, the glass must go into a special programmable kiln called an annealer. The annealer allows the glass to cool evenly and completely. This process gives the glass additional strength and durability. Without the process in the annealer, the glass is prone to cracking and breaking with the lightest of bumps, or the glass may even shatter spontaneously for no apparent reason.

As a target of workplace bullying, you too have been under tremendous stress and pressure. Just like the "cooling off period" that glass must go through in the annealer to become strong and durable, so must you. Take the time to care for yourself. Bring your mental and physical self to the point where you feel "tougher." Your situation is unique to you, but you are not alone. You are now part of a select group of savvier, wiser, and stronger people who have had their lives shaped by the heat of workplace bullying. Take the time and make the effort to build your confidence and resilience back up. You are worth it.

Reflection Questions

The reflection questions for this step will help you purge the negative messages that the bully put in your head and replace them with positive, confidence-building thoughts.

1) What words and emotions do you need to purge? Write your letter to the bully and choose your favorite method of destruction!

2) How will you recall your success? Make a list of your successes. Consider framing your list and keeping it on your

desk or nightstand so you can look at it each day. It doesn't need to become part of your permanent decor, but keep it visible for a while as a reminder.

3) What activities will you prioritize to build resilience? Download the resilience calendar from the workbook and select activities weekly that will help you build resilience.

4) What about your experience with bullying has made you a stronger person? Write a letter to yourself. Explain to your future self that despite the challenges, you emerged more resilient. Consider sealing your letter in an envelope and putting it somewhere you can open it and look at it one year from now to reflect on how far you have come.

Step Seven – Letting Go

Moving Forward Stronger and Wiser

Step Six addressed why it's important for you to intentionally take time to rebuild your confidence and resilience. Step Seven examines those leftover feelings that can hang on long after we've left the bully behind. How do you move past feelings of loss, anger, and even feelings of revenge? How do you let go when the feelings are so strong? If you don't move past these feelings, they can certainly continue to impact your job performance and relationships, and possibly even your health.

I've mentioned feelings of grief several times in the book already. Being a target of workplace bullying can lead to a loss of self, loss of sense of safety in the workplace, and of course, loss of job or income. Understanding the sense of loss involved in the changes surrounding your situation is key to being able to move forward. If your grief is preventing you from moving forward, consider seeking a counselor who specializes in grief. They can help you understand your unique orientation to loss and help you process your feelings surrounding your experience. I'm an advocate of The Grief Recovery Method. Grief Recovery is a specific process designed to help you move through not just traditional grief, but any loss (relationship, job, faith, health, finances, etc.).[24] Learn more about this method by engaging the resources listed in the back of the book.

---

24   John W. James and Russell Friedman, *The Grief Recovery Handbook: The Action Program for Moving Beyond Death, Divorce, and Other Losses* (New York: Harper-Collins Publishers, 2009).

You might experience feelings of revenge. I certainly felt vengeful after both of my encounters. I honestly can't think of any other time in my life where I wanted to seek revenge on people who hurt me, but I did want revenge on my bullies. Holding onto feelings of vengeance certainly isn't healthy, and letting go of that emotion is crucial for moving on.

There was a time in my life when I would've said I would *never* forgive my bullies, but I realized that the bullies had moved on. They were not thinking about me or my situation anymore. Forgiveness is for you, not others. Being hesitant to forgive will hold you back from truly moving beyond your experience.

To move forward, I had to take intentional action to let go and forgive. I won't lie—this was some of the hardest emotional work I've ever done. But I can tell you it's worth it. I encourage you to move toward a place where you can emotionally put this experience in your rearview mirror. If you can successfully work through the feelings of loss and revenge and come to a place of forgiveness, you'll become a stronger and wiser professional.

Story - The Phone Call

After my Deceiver experience, I often dragged myself to my new job. I spent time most evenings crying, wondering why and how it had all gone so wrong. I talked about it constantly to friends and family. I seesawed between being sad then angry, then back to sadness and depression. I was once again not myself. I didn't like it, but I couldn't let go.

One Sunday night, I was upset (again), so I called my mom. For more than a year since I had left my job, my parents were my constant supporters. They patiently listened to me, consoled me, and did everything in their power to build me back up. I expected no difference from this phone call to my mom. I expected that I would talk (and probably cry), and she would patiently listen and give some words of encouragement at the end of our conversation. When I explained why I was upset (again) she said, "Dawn, I don't know how else I can help you. You need to stop thinking about it and move forward. I will talk to you later. Goodbye." Then she hung up the phone. At first, I was in disbelief. My mother had just hung up on me! She left me to cry by myself all alone.

Upon reflection, the act of stopping me from wallowing (again) was the kindest and most loving thing she could have done for me at that point. More than a year had passed, and I was still ruminating and focusing precious time being upset about a situation I couldn't change. My aggressors were no longer focused on me, yet I was still focused on them. My mom's words opened my eyes to the fact that I needed to take intentional action to move forward. It would be hard. I had focused so many of my thoughts and so much of my energy toward this situation, but she was right. I needed to let go.

Moving Forward

When can you move on? What is the appropriate amount of time to grieve, process, and stew? Every person is different, so there's no one right answer here. As humans, we can hold on to things for a *long* time—long after it is healthy to do so. Yet some of us will attempt to just walk away and immediately put the past behind us without processing the situation. So too little processing isn't healthy, but too much stewing will start eroding your quality of life.

Workplace bullying is the most difficult and traumatic experience that I've ever faced in the workplace, and as I have already shared, this experience spilled out into my personal life. Workplace bullies steal so much from the target. There's a lot of loss to process, but when you sit back and reflect, there's a lot to gain as well. If you don't at least take some time to process, you're missing out on the hidden benefit of being a target. You will learn about yourself, about others, and in time, you might find that moving away from the bully meant moving toward something even better.

In the end, moving forward is a conscious decision. A decision to think about something else. A decision to talk about something else. I needed a little shove to start my process. You may need a shove too. Who in your support network will give you a little tough love and tell you when it's time to move on when you seem to be stuck?

To arrive at the point where you feel you can let go of the experience, try identifying lessons you learned, practicing gratitude, and forgiving the bully. These are powerful tools that can move your brain into the right frame of mind so you can move forward.

Learning Lessons

Identifying the lessons you need to learn from a bullying situation is one of the most challenging exercises you'll tackle. It is also one of the most worthwhile. Even during our most painful experiences, we can learn lessons that can help us be a better professional and a better person. Here are a few of the lessons I learned:

- If someone is talking to me about other people, they are more than likely talking to others about me.
- I can't assume that people around me know what I have accomplished. I need to advocate for myself and even brag a little bit from time to time.
- Trust takes years to build but can be shattered in a moment.
- Trust your instincts because when something feels off, your instincts are probably right.

One of the first things you can identify is what you know now about bullying that you didn't know before. How developed is your Bully Intelligence? Will you recognize the signs in the future? How might you mitigate the damage if you found yourself in the situation again? How might you be able to intervene if you saw it happening to someone else?

You are not to blame for becoming a target, but it might be important to identify the behaviors that didn't serve you well in this situation. Think back to my story about my tears in the workplace. Maybe you have been expressing emotions or words that unintentionally inflame the situation? How will you redirect those behaviors in a future situation? Do you know something now that you'll implement going forward to prevent another bullying encounter? You didn't create the negative situation you are in, but that doesn't mean that you can't create a positive resolution. Take the lessons you learned. Leverage them to help others and benefit yourself.

Practicing Gratitude

It may be too soon after your bully encounter to discuss being grateful for your experience, but I can tell you that upon reflection, I'm grateful for both of my encounters. Yes, I said it—*grateful*. It took time for me to see the positive side, but reframing my experience was a key part of my healing.

Start by building small levels of gratitude. You may be grateful for your ability to navigate the situation, or you may be grateful for your new job. Over time, your gratitude may expand. Start a gratitude journal focused on this incident.

After my grad school experience, I wrote letters to the people from my grad school community who positively influenced my time there—my landlords, one of my professors, and a couple of my grad school friends. To really pull out the positives, directing myself to write a letter helped me to find the little slivers of good in what was largely a negative experience. I am grateful for many things related to my bullying experience, not the least of which is that I can write this book and that I have the privilege to work with and support amazing professionals like you.

My gratitude extends to the things I learned about my own strength and character. I'm proud of the strength that it took me to advocate for myself in graduate school. As a rule, I am conflict avoidant, but I stood strong when I saw injustice being done to me (and others), despite the conflict.

On the heels of the Deceiver bully, I went back to grad school. I was interested in studying organizational culture, effective workplaces, and leadership. My default when something goes awry is to try to learn and diagnose what went wrong. I went on to earn two master's degrees focused on business leadership and organizational change. I don't believe I would have pursued those degrees (at least not when I did) if it were not for my experiences. My coursework was much more meaningful to me because I had lived experience of workplace dysfunction that others had not. The work that I do with leaders in my current job is personal. I know how much leadership matters. I hope that I help my leaders create better environments for their employees.

When I left my job, I went on to do work that I probably

would have never considered doing. I met good friends at those workplaces that I never would have met otherwise. I began to study the elements of workplace trust and now have developed a regional reputation for speaking and teaching on the topic. Right now, it may feel like nothing good can come out of this situation. But trust me, you will be able to look back and see what you know, have, and can do, all because of a bully.

Finding Forgiveness

When I talk with other targets, some say they won't ever forgive their bully. I once heard not forgiving someone is like putting poison in your own coffee every day but hoping that the other person will die. Forgiving someone doesn't mean you're condoning the behavior. Forgiveness is for yourself. Offering forgiveness (or not) does not help (or harm) your aggressor either way. Being able to forgive marks the passage from the angry vengeful you to the person who is at peace with the experience. You become a person who is ready to take the lessons forward and leave the rest behind.

You must also forgive yourself. On some level you may still have shame and self-blame circling you. Forgive yourself for whatever role you played (or thought you played) in exacerbating or prolonging the situation.

During my experience with the Deceiver bully, I remember having a conversation with my brother. We didn't talk regularly, but he knew how much I loved my job and was surprised when I told him I was looking for something new. I shared with him the CliffsNotes version of what had happened, and I remember saying to him tearfully, "I feel so dumb. How could I let someone ruin my reputation and destroy this position for me? How could I let this happen?"

At the time, my brother worked with children who had severe mental health issues. After hearing my story, he said, "You can't blame yourself. If this person was a child at my center, we would most likely diagnose them with a personality disorder. *Normal, mentally healthy people just don't do things like that to other people.* You (and others) were manipulated, and you can't blame yourself for that." His words lifted a weight off my shoulders. I needed to let go of the blame and forgive myself before moving on.

In your journey, you may discover additional steps or practices that help you move forward. As you move into the final step (number eight), which is about telling your story, I encourage you to share your lessons and practices with others so all targets can benefit.

Reflection Questions

The questions for this step lay the groundwork for the final step—telling your story. Key aspects of telling your story will be about lessons learned and how you helped yourself mentally move past the experience. You can use the "Telling Your Story Template" in the companion workbook to record your thoughts or use a personal journal if you have one.

1) List at least two lessons learned that you can think of right now because of your bully encounter. There may be more lessons in the future. Continue adding to your list as they emerge.

2) Write down one thing you are grateful for about your experience. Try to expand your list by one more "grateful for" each week over four weeks.

3) Are you ready to forgive? Is there anything you need/want to forgive yourself for? Bless and release any actions you feel you need for self-forgiveness. When will you forgive the bully? Some people find comfort by writing their statement of forgiveness on a helium balloon and releasing it. Alternatively, write it on a rock and throw the rock into water. Pick a time and date that you will let go and forgive.

Step Eight – Telling Your Story

Empowering Yourself and Others

The two previous steps were all about healing and intentionally moving forward emotionally. You've reached Step Eight, and now I'm giving you some unconventional advice: *Tell your story.*

Targets of workplace bullies typically keep their stories to themselves. Why am I encouraging you to share what could be one of the most traumatic experiences of your career? By sharing our stories, we can demonstrate to the world that workplace bullying does occur and that it can happen to anyone. We can shake off the stigma when we openly explain our experience, and we dispel the myth that targets are flawed or somehow encouraged the abuse.

What has stopped us from telling our stories until now? Our shame and embarrassment prevent us from sharing, and in turn, we continue to protect the bully. Now you know the truth about why you were targeted. Remember the positive, responsible, experienced employee that you are. Don't let shame and embarrassment stop you. Even if you had some moments you aren't proud of during your experience, you did nothing wrong.

Perhaps you fear repercussions for you or your career if you tell your story. But telling our story in the spirit of helping others, and not with a spirit of revenge, does matter. We can tell our story in a way that doesn't identify our workplace or the bully, but instead helps others who have been targeted. Stories help others build their Bully Intelligence.

We underestimate the power of our story. I learned the power of my story just a couple of years ago. If I hadn't told my story, a dear friend would have continued to live in shame and self-blame, feeling totally alone in her experience.

Story - It Happened to Me Too

One weekend I was out of town with some girlfriends. Many of these friends had heard both of my workplace bullying stories. During one conversation, I was recounting just a small part of the Deceiver bully story. I suddenly became aware that one of my friends stopped what she was doing. As she listened to me tell the story, tears formed in her eyes. When I paused, she said, "I can't believe that happened to you. You are such a professional person. How could someone do that to you? Do you know what happened to me?"

I didn't know what had happened to her. She proceeded to tell me her story, one that had eerily similar elements to mine.

Not unlike most targets, my friend had assumed she'd done something wrong to bring the situation upon herself. This same group of friends had been together many times since her experience. We've known each other for years. We know and trust each other, yet she hadn't said anything. Maybe she assumed we wouldn't believe her. Perhaps she thought we would view her differently if we knew.

When she heard my story, she had a "me too" moment. She realized she was not the only one. If she had not heard my story that day, she would have never revealed the truth about her experience.

Unfortunately, because of the bully's treatment, and subsequently her supervisor's, my friend was forced to leave her position. Like many other targets, her financial position became precarious as she sought other employment. She had earned a master's degree in her field and had years of experience that granted her the privilege of performing her work at a high level. I'm not sure my friend will ever go back to the career she loved because of the trauma caused by this incident.

When I'm asked who this book is for, I think of my friend and all the others like her who think they are alone. Targets who still feel pangs of blame, shame, fear, and self-doubt. Targets who are either still wrestling to get away from their aggressor or who are still psychologically in the grasp of their aggressor.

Telling your story may not seem like a proper step to take on the surface, but hear me out. Telling your story can be cathartic for you. For many years, only my parents and a few close friends had heard both of my stories. I held back because I still had the belief that I had done something wrong or that I had done something to cause the situation. After much reflection, I came to the realization that I had done nothing wrong and that the persons who should be ashamed were my aggressors. Yet writing this book is the first time I am telling this story outside of my small group of confidants. It's been twenty-five years since my first experience and more than a decade since the second, yet this is the first time many of my colleagues and acquaintances will hear my stories.

When we get to the point where we can tell our story from a place of strength, it can be incredibly empowering. By revealing our story, we can make others more aware that these situations occur in the workplace. Hopefully we can help others start to recognize patterns of behavior earlier and we can prevent some of these situations. We also let aggressors know that we won't be hiding their secrets anymore, and we tell organizations that we are savvy and capable of helping them disarm the workplace bullies.

Tell Your Story When You Are Ready

For me, talking to others always helps me move past strong, painful emotions. I told my story to one or two people I immediately wished I had not told, mainly because they believed that no one would act that way toward someone without provocation. But most people I told fully believed and supported me. By default, I became the person they came to when they had their own unsettling experiences at work. This is where I learned the power of my story could help not only me but also others.

If you just escaped an abusive workplace situation, I can tell you from experience that you might share with a close relative or friend, but you won't be ready to share your story with a broader group of people. Getting some distance between you and the situation helps. The other thing you'll need to do is build yourself back up and regain your footing in whatever you choose to do next—getting a new job, starting a new business, retiring, etc.

When you can tell your story and not feel overwhelming amounts of sadness or rage, that's a good indicator that you might be ready. Those emotions will always be present in some amount when you recount your story, but if you do the emotional work to heal and rebuild your confidence, those emotions won't knock you to your knees.

Tell Your Story for the Right Reasons

When telling your story, it's critical that you always tell it for the right reasons. Telling your story out of anger or revenge only makes you seem less credible. The aggressor was in the wrong, but you do not need to give the aggressor a reason to make you a target outside of the workplace. Even though your story is true and you're stating facts, don't tempt the bully to tie you up in a legal mess. That will only serve to retraumatize you and detract from your healing process. Remember that success is the best revenge.

As targets, we often inadvertently protect the aggressor because we're hesitant to reveal anything to anybody for fear of being judged or blamed by others. Telling your story sets you free of that "protecting" mode (even if you're not revealing the aggressor's name).

From very early on in your healing process, you'll most likely start telling your story as a means to engage support for yourself. The first people you share with will most likely be your therapist and your best friend, and maybe you'll choose to stop there. Other targets may choose to write a blog post, tell it on a podcast, or write a book. Choose the method that feels right for you.

Tell Your Story to Empower Yourself and Others

Sharing my story led people back to me when they needed help thinking through their own situations. As a talented, intelligent professional, you can demonstrate that anyone could be a potential target, regardless of level of degree, numbers of years of experience, and industry. Even more importantly, you can serve as a model of someone who navigated their way through it and continued to be a successful professional on the other side. You can let people know that they aren't alone. You can create a safe space—a sense of community—for others.

Only those who have had bullying experiences can truly understand what we have been through. We are smarter, savvier, and more perceptive thanks to our experience. We have learned lessons that no one else will understand, and we can share those lessons from a place of strength and wisdom like no one else.

Before you tell your story to a broader audience, it's critical that you take time to examine what you learned from the experience. What did you learn about yourself? What did you learn about other people? What will you do differently in the future based on what you learned? What would you encourage others to do? What have you gained that you wouldn't have if it weren't for this bullying experience? Is there anything you are grateful for after having the experience?

It might take you a while, perhaps several years, to realize what you have gained. But you *will* get there. Keep reflecting and rebuilding, and you'll be able to look back and see the positive.

I have a quote on my computer wallpaper right now: "You have been preparing all your life for *this* moment." I used to think about my experience in grad school as just an unfortunate blip in my journey. It was maybe a sign that I wasn't meant to go down the path of grad school that early or in that topic area. I now see *that* moment as the start of my intended journey. Before I could even imagine I'd work with leaders and employees, my experience uniquely prepared me to fulfill this role. I often describe my ten months in grad school as the hardest year of my life. But I've also always described it as a year of great learning. Learning about myself, about other people, and about the dark side of the working world. As hard as that year was, I don't regret my decision to go to school that year.

Embrace your story. Your story and how you survived is now a part of who you are. You will take the strength and lessons that you've built through this experience, and you will use them to benefit yourself and others.

Reflection Questions

This set of reflection questions will prepare you to tell your story. For additional brainstorming questions and ideas on how to tell your story, refer to the workbook.

1) What are the reasons you want to tell your story?
2) What lessons will you share when you tell your story?
3) How will you know when you are emotionally ready to share your story? Can you tell your story without getting emotional?
4) Who will you share your story with? Start with a friend or family member, then decide if there are other people (or places) where you want to share.

Final Encouragement from the Author

I wrote this book with big, bold goals—to help targets of bullying reclaim their careers, rebuild their confidence, and break free from the psychological hold of the bully. I know change doesn't occur overnight, and based on my own experience, I know that transformation can take years. I hope that my story has inspired you to start down the path toward your own transformation.

Start by taking action. Don't wait another minute to plan your departure. The bully won't suddenly wake up one day and start being nice to you. They aren't going to change. You are the one who must make the move to change. Unfair, I know, but remember you never know where this change will take you. You can find another path or position that you adore, maybe even more than your current position. The excitement of pursuing something new alongside new colleagues awaits you. You can do it!

Prioritize yourself by taking the time to manage your stress and mental health. Create your resilience practice and make room in your day for exercise and fresh air. Take the time to rebuild your confidence. You are worth every minute you put into restoring you.

Share your story. There is absolutely nothing to be ashamed about. Wear your experience like a badge of honor. You learned in this book that you were targeted not because you were weak, but because you were a potential *threat*. Think about that. You are so good at what you do, you have so much power and influence, you are so popular at work that someone felt the need to go to great lengths to take you out. Tell your story with that same level of confidence that your power and influence emanate.

Your journey from where you are emotionally or career wise today could take some time. There will be points along the way where you'll feel stuck. Remember that you can always return to the reflection questions and exercises at the end of each chapter or in the companion workbook. Revisiting a question after additional time has passed may make the reflection more meaningful and enhance insights to keep you moving forward.

Sharing my story with friends, and now with you in this book, has been one of the most transformative experiences in my journey. Some people have asked me how I feel about having my name forever linked to the concept of workplace bullying. I have pondered that all throughout the writing of this book. I attempted two other times to write about these experiences, but it either wasn't the right time emotionally or I was doing it for the wrong reasons. I just couldn't do it. But now is the time. I can say without a doubt that I am honored to have my name forever linked to this concept. Not because I was bullied, but because I have now passed along lessons and tools to support you. I hope you find that sharing your story is as empowering, liberating, and enlightening as it was for me.

Although we've come to the end of the book, it does not need to be the end of our journey together. As I reached the final stages of writing this book, I knew I wanted to begin building a community for people who had experienced workplace bullying. A safe space where we could share stories and continue to build our Bully Intelligence. For that reason, I've created a Facebook Group, the Outwit the Workplace Bully Community. In the community, you'll find supportive individuals who share everything from how to deal with difficult people at work to job search tips. I invite you to join us! We can outwit the bully and move forward confidently together.

Congratulations on taking the time to invest in yourself by reading this book. Thank you for allowing me to share all I have learned with you. Continue to advocate for yourself, your health, and your career. I wish you all the best. You deserve it!

Additional Resources

Learn more about workplace bullying, the research, and additional resources available by visiting the Workplace Bullying Institute online or by reading the book *The Bully at Work* written by WBI Director, Gary Namie.

Website:

https://workplacebullying.org/

Book:

The Bully at Work: What You Can Do to Stop the Hurt and Reclaim Your Dignity on the Job by Gary Namie, PhD and Ruth Namie, PhD

Find information and support on managing your mental health by visiting the National Alliance on Mental Illness (NAMI). Engage in online support groups and discussions, watch videos, and read articles on a variety of topics. You can even find NAMI resources specific to your state.

https://www.nami.org/Home

Get help right on your phone with BetterHelp. Start by getting matched with a licensed therapist, then communicate your way through messaging, chat, phone, or video. BetterHelp is a weekly membership that you can cancel anytime.

https://www.betterhelp.com/

Talkspace offers access to licensed therapists through messaging, phone, or video sessions. They offer several subscription options based on your needs, and your subscription can be canceled anytime.

https://try.talkspace.com/

Design your own resilience toolkit through Mental Health First Aid of Canada:

COVID-19 Self-Care and Resilience Guide

https://www.mhfa.ca/en/blog/mental-health-first-aid-covid-19-self-care-resilience-guide

Explore the concept of resilience alongside other helpful topics such as stress, mindfulness, gratitude, happiness, forgiveness, etc., by visiting the University of California, Berkeley Greater Good Science Center (GGSC). GGSC sponsors scientific research and explores effective practices around social and emotional well-being.

GGSC Online

https://www.greatergood.berkeley.edu/

Explore the sense of loss by either reading *The Grief Recovery Handbook* or by finding a grief recovery specialist in your area using the link below.

Book:

The Grief Recovery Handbook: The Action Program for Moving Beyond Death, Divorce, and Other Losses by John W. James and Russell Friedman

https://www.griefrecoverymethod.com/books

Website:

https://www.griefrecoverymethod.com/

If you're struggling to find a new position in your geographic area, check out FlexJobs.com. Members pay an affordable membership fee to access their database of thousands of legitimate and fully vetted remote and flexible jobs. Entry-level to executive-level jobs available. Articles and webinars are also available for support during the various phases of the job search.

https://www.flexjobs.com/

Acknowledgments

One thing I have learned through the process of writing this book is that while drafting may be a solitary pursuit, publishing a book is not. It takes a great team of experts and champions.

Writing a book, let alone publishing a book, was not on my original list of goals for 2021. I wouldn't have achieved this accomplishment without the help of the team at Self-Publishing School (SPS). Thank you for putting together a comprehensive and inspiring experience for learning to self-publish. To my SPS coach, Kerk Murray, thank you for being both advisor and cheerleader. To the SPS community who show up every day, thank you for every post and for generating such positivity and camaraderie!

To my editor, Val Cervarich, thank you for making publishing for the first time both enriching and enjoyable.

To the "Sunday Card Crew," thanks for putting up with my absence from the weekly card game when I was up against a deadline.

To my dad, Norm, you were excited about this book from the moment I told you I was going to write it. I know Mom would be excited too. Thank you for all the love and support you have shown me throughout my life and for raising me to be a kind human being.

To my brother, Scott, for encouraging me to rethink my role in the experience and inspiring the Finding Forgiveness section of the book. Thank you for always being there for me.

To my friends and family who approached my declaration "I'm writing a book" with enthusiasm and support. Many of you recounted your own stories of toxic relationships in the workplace and helped me to refine my advice, so thank you! Last, but not least, to my dear friend for inspiring Step Eight and for allowing me to share your moment of revelation.

When it comes to having a team of supporters, I have the best!

About the Author

Dawn is an author, speaker, and the founder of On the Rise Development, LLC. As an advocate for thriving workplaces, Dawn has dedicated more than a decade to helping leaders and employees grow in their careers.

She earned her BA in psychology along with a Master of Business Administration and a Master of Arts in Management, all from The College of St. Scholastica.

When she's not writing, you might find Dawn capturing family memories in a scrapbook, losing at a game of Hand and Foot, or cheering for her niece and nephew at the ballfield or ice rink. She resides in northern Minnesota.

To learn more about Dawn and On the Rise Development, visit www.ontherisedevelopment.com.

Did you find this book helpful?

Please leave a review!

I am on a mission to help as many people as I can escape the grip of workplace bullying.

Every review matters. Your review matters. Help me reach more people by providing your insights on how my book helped you.

Head over to Amazon (or wherever you purchased this book) and leave an honest review.

Thank you in advance!

www.ingramcontent.com/pod-product-compliance
Lightning Source LLC
Chambersburg PA
CBHW060539130626
46553CB00002B/828

* 9 7 9 8 9 8 5 2 1 3 2 0 1 *